AF572244

HOME AND SCHOOL:
EARLY LANGUAGE AND READING

HOME AND SCHOOL: EARLY LANGUAGE AND READING

edited by
Bryant Fillion
Carolyn N. Hedley
Emily C. DiMartino

Fordham University

Ablex Publishing Corporation
Norwood, New Jersey 07648

Printed in the United States of America

Library of Congress Cataloging-in-Publication Data

Home and school.

Bibliography: p.
Includes indexes.
1. Children—Language. 2. Language acquisition.
3. Language arts. 4. Home and school. I. Fillion, Bryant, 1938– II. Hedley, Carolyn N.
III. DiMartino, Emily C. (Emily Comstock)
LB1139.L3H643 1987 372.6 87-14319
ISBN 0-89391-421-5

Ablex Publishing Corporation
355 Chestnut St.
Norwood, New Jersey 07648

Table of Contents

To our children,
who bring our thoughts to life:
Helen Fillion
Katy Fillion
John Hedley
Nicholas DiMartino
Catherine DiMartino

The Authors

GLENDA BISSEX. Glenda Bissex is on the faculty of Northeastern University, as well as Norwich University in Vermont. Primarily, however, Glenda Bissex is a writer, who can teach and write about writing. She began her work by discovering how her own son came to learn about the world of the written word, described in *GNYS AT WRK: A child learns to write and read*. Her doctorate is from Harvard Graduate School of Education, and she has degrees from the University of Chicago and from Radcliffe. She has taught English at Newton High School in Massachusetts and Francis W. Parker School in Chicago. Currently she is writing, with Jeanne Chall, a book on holistic assessment of text.

ANGELA CARRASQUILLO. Angela Carrasquillo is an associate professor at Fordham University, where she is coordinator of the Teaching English to Speakers of Other Languages (TESOL) Program. Dr. Carrasquillo is a prolific writer: She has written two books in the area of teaching reading to the bilingual student; she has written several monographs on the Neo-Rican, and she is nationally known in the area of bilingual education. Dr. Carrasquillo has degrees from the University of Puerto Rico and a Ph.D. from New York University.

EMILY C. DIMARTINO. Emily DiMartino is an adjunct professor at Fordham University and at Manhattan Community College, where she teaches in the early childhood programs. She has taught minicourses at the Spence School in Manhattan; she has worked as a classroom teacher for the Head Start Program and she has directed bilingual-monolingual programs in elementary education, coordinating evaluation, in the Bilingual Education Service Center at Hunter College. Dr. DiMartino received degrees from Syracuse University and her Ph.D. from Fordham University.

BRYANT FILLION. Bryant Fillion is the head of the doctoral program in language, literacy, and learning at Fordham University. His international contacts in the areas of language development and literacy aided us in engaging some of the ranking researchers for the Reading/ Early Childhood Institute. Dr. Fillion teaches courses in language development, the cognitive bases of reading, and psycholinguistics. He has degrees from the University of Michigan, Long Island University, the University of Illinois, and a doctorate from Florida State University. Dr. Fillion has coauthored several books, including *Teaching English today*, the *Inquiry into literature* series, and *Writing for results*.

MARJORIE GROSETT. Marjorie Grosett, executive director of the Day Care Council of New York, is the consummate hands-on practitioner: For most of her professional life, she has worked in the area of day care. She not only brought up her own children well, she was highly concerned for the children of others and she worked on the Day Care Council of New York for many years until her recent retirement. As executive director, her will prevailed regarding standards and procedures in the somewhat unregulated area of day care, where much of the programmatic activity had been plainly custodial. Thus, she was a pioneer in New York State for setting standards and for insisting on quality educational day care; later, she was a consultant to the federal government in this area. She is widely respected for her historic contributions to day care programs.

CAROLYN N. HEDLEY. Carolyn N. Hedley is an associate professor and director of reading programs at the Fordham University Graduate School of Education. She has been involved in the development of the doctoral program in language literacy and learning at Fordham and in the masters program in early childhood education. Dr. Hedley is coeditor of the book, *Contexts of reading* and she has published widely in journals of reading (e.g., *Reading Horizons, Educational and Psychological Measurement, Elementary English*). She has contributed articles to several books, on such topics as career education and the language arts and reading difficulties. Dr. Hedley is a coauthor of Scott Foresman's *Lifelong series in adult education: Reading comprehension*, which includes 24 books. Dr. Hedley received a doctorate from the University of Illinois.

IRENE SHIGAKI. Irene Shigaki is an associate professor at New York University, where she directs the infant and toddler education program. She also directs the doctoral program in early childhood and elementary education at New York University. Dr. Shigaki has done copious research on infant, toddler, and preschool education in Japan. She has written extensively in such journals as *Young Children, Child Study Journal*, and *Gifted Child Quarterly*. Dr. Shigaki holds degrees from the University of Washington, Seattle; she received a doctorate from Teachers College,

Columbia University. She taught at Columbia University and at Montclair State College before coming to New York University.

DENNY TAYLOR. Denny Taylor thinks of herself as primarily a writer—a writer of ethnographic studies of children, of poetry, and of children's books. Her work involves systematic ways of looking at children and at literacy as a sociocultural phenomenon which has consequences for and is affected by family and community life. A senior research fellow at Teachers College, Columbia University, she is nearly always engrossed in field work while she is writing. Dr. Taylor has written *Family literacy: Young children learning to read and to write, Family storybook reading*, and *Growing up literate*. She has contributed many chapters to books and many articles to journals. Dr. Taylor has degrees from Whitelands College, London University Institute of Education, and Rutgers University; she received a doctorate from Teachers College, Columbia University.

GORDON WELLS. Currently, Gordon Wells is a professor at the Ontario Institute for Studies in Education. Before coming to OISE, he was research director for the Center of the Study of Language and Communication of the University of Bristol. From his work there came the well-known Bristol study, described in *Learning through interaction: The study of language development*, a seminal study in the area of language development. A second book, *Language development in the preschool years*, was followed by a third, *The meaning makers: Children learning language and using language to learn*, reporting on further developments and insights from the study. These three volumes have provided on-going reports of the longitudinal research from Wells's seminal Bristol work. Dr. Wells is continuing his research, using Canadian children, looking at cross-cultural similarities and differences. Dr. Wells was the Early Childhood Institute's keynote speaker; he fascinated his audience for 4 hours a day for 2 days; thus, we asked him to be our keynote author as well. His writing proves to be as stimulating as his speech!

Preface

Remember the anecdote of the Bowery panhandler who wore the sign "I owe $250,000 in back rent and I'm a quarter short"? There was a touch of that same spirit when it came time to finish this volume. We had a fine time organizing and running Fordham University's Reading/Early Childhood Institute, where earlier versions of these papers were presented in 1985. The speakers were enthusiastic; the tapes were clear; the transcriptions were in order. However, formulating each chapter was more arduous. Our authors would submit their work and then begin rethinking their chapters. Then they would ask for them to be returned; revision would occur and then more revision. Just before our deadline, we were all able to find the quarter to make the payment, finally coming up with the volume before you.

Despite differing topics and emphases, the authors here maintain a consistent view of language development and use at home and school, a view that may not be consonant with current practice in some early childhood programs. First, we look at language development of the young child and its role in the child's learning, schooling, and mental development. How do children learn language so quickly and what form does language learning take? How do children's preschool language experiences influence subsequent school performance? In addressing these general questions, we consider the practical issues related to the parts that parents, teachers, and other caregivers play in children's language, intellectual development and school performance. In these chapters, we are saying that in natural ways, children can learn a great deal more from the environment when parents and teachers serve as mediators between children's experiences and their learning—particularly language learning.

The philosophy underlying the institute and this volume is that language growth occurs through interaction, that children need and naturally want to become language users, that contexts and strategies are important in this development, and that early reading and writing are natural extensions of children's language development in a literate culture. Language use and development are fostered at both home and school; stress on how the home and school can work together in this enterprise was a primary concern of the institute's organizers and speakers.

Practical implications of theory and research were developed for home, day care centers, and schools in workshops and discussion groups following each author's presentation to the institute. Topics for discussion included the administration of effective early childhood education programs; issues and practices in infant and toddler programs; early language development in home and school; play, language, and mental development; cognitive development of the young child; books for young children, and parenting practices with young children.

The graduate students who participated in the institute were for the most part practitioners. Question sessions following the major presentations were exhilarating, humorous, and realistic. The workshop discussions were delightful, productive, and practical; several student papers were themselves highly publishable. Unfortunately, the questions, discussions, and student papers could not be included in this volume, though some participant discussion has been retained in Marjorie Grossett's chapter. A nice light tone seemed to infuse the conference; perhaps it was the central subject—the very young child—that caused an optimistic, hopeful, and highly professional mood to prevail. One cannot be very cynical when one is dealing with the very young. Their potential and the potential of the high-tech times in which we live force us to respect the future that is bound to be astounding. We hope that this volume will contribute to that future, both for the children, and for those who care for and teach them.

It is in contemplating the future of our children that we decided to dedicate the book to our own children. However, we also wish to thank the many people who helped us: first of all, our authors, who were more responsive and responsible than we dared to hope; and then, Anne Goldstein, who typed the manuscript and helped us clear up the details. Finally, our thanks to our families and friends, who have learned to put up with the stress of publication deadlines.

Bryant Fillion
Carolyn Hedley
Emily DiMartino
June 1987

Introduction

The chapters in this book began as presentations in 1985 at Fordham University's Reading/Early Childhood Institute. Like the institute, the book is organized into two parts: The first deals with various aspects of language development, including its graphic manifestations and its social dimensions; the second part deals with the context in which language develops: the social and cultural milieu and the kinds of schooling that may foster or hinder language development.

Gordon Wells was the institute's keynote speaker; his opening two chapters set the tone for this book as well. He maintains that from infancy children are active participants in a social experience, actively constructing meaning, their language, and their own knowledge. The adult as mediator between learners and their experiences is essential to these constructive processes. Adults can be more effective in interacting with children when they, too, construct new knowledge about the child as the child learns. Dr. Wells sets forth principles which will help the adult participant to interact productively with the young learner in the home and classroom, by observing rather than being didactic. In the second chapter, Dr. Wells suggests that learning to read uses many of the same principles involved in learning to speak; thus preschool experiences that lead to literacy can be provided. It is important, for example, that children understand the functions of written language and learn at an early age to direct their own thought processes. Dr. Wells provides models for four levels of literacy teaching, and discusses the influence of each on language teaching and learning. Wells suggests efficient literacy practices for the classroom, emphasizing the vital role of the teacher in aiding children to use and learn from written language.

In Chapter 3, Glenda Bissex discusses beginning writing, further developing the notion of negotiated meaning that had been introduced by Wells. She begins her chapter with a description of a primitive literacy event, from a story by Rudyard Kipling. Dr. Bissex indicates that writing develops as an extension of oral language, which often precedes and informs written forms of language. She demonstrates that written language is fostered by enchantment with the word, that writing can bring a great deal of pleasure to children, and that teachers should enjoy writing with children. Heavily didactic teaching and red pencil revision tactics are clearly *not* a desirable part of the process when beginning writing occurs. Carolyn Hedley, in Chapter 4, discusses "hands-on" home and classroom literacy practices that foster the reading and writing of even very young children. Following the presentation of specific techniques, consonant with the theory and principles introduced in the previous chapters, Dr. Hedley discusses the change of parenting patterns from the nuclear family to present-day family arrangements. She argues that all forms of early childhood education and care should provide children with the experience of rich literacy environments.

Emily DiMartino, in Chapter 5, discusses language development in the social and moral development of young children. In developing her own research and using studies from Gilligan, Pool, Schweder, and Much, Dr. DiMartino points out that children understand the various levels of moral and social interaction, as well as the power and significance of social behaviors. Dr. DiMartino derives her information from the conversation of children; she points out that children are very savvy about the social life in which they participate and she suggests that adults must recognize this in order to increase their credibility when they communicate with children.

The final chapter in this section was written by Denny Taylor, who explores the world of childhood and the thinking of young children. She presents an interpretive model of the (con)textual worlds of childhood, extolling that part of children's thinking which is irrationally significant. Her model derives from adults' memories of childhood and the talk and writings of children. It is important for us to rediscover the alternative dimensions of childhood experience that we have learned to ignore and may long since have forgotten. There is a poetic sense of the real magic of childhood in her chapter.

Part II of this volume is concerned with the contexts of language development. Irene Shigaki, in Chapter 7, writes about the transmission of values in Japanese day care centers. We considered placing this chapter in Part I because of its similarity to Dr. DiMartino's line of thought regarding the language of social regulation. But clearly, what Dr. Shigaki was discussing was the milieu, in this case Japanese day care, in which values are imparted. She speaks less about the language of values and more about the cultural means of influencing values. Dr. Shigaki powerfully makes the point that a great many value-related concepts are developed in infancy and toddlerhood when the child's language competence is in its formative stage. Language is a potent factor in values transmission; but in Japan, many of the social constructs which foster the development of values occur in ways that are not verbal.

Angela Carrasquillo, in Chapter 8, discusses bilingualism and its effects on language development, learning, and cognition. She maintains that the issue of early language learning in terms of mastering a second language has not been resolved. There is little in the literature to suggest that early acquisition, when learning languages sequentially, benefits the learner in terms of mastery. There is a great deal of research which indicates that there is a positive relationship between bilingualism and cognitive development. Following a review of various theories and research, Dr. Carrasquillo finds that learning a second language does not impede learning in a first language and may have a positive effect on children's cognitive development.

Marjorie Grossett discusses the nature and problems of day care in our society. Her chapter deals with the goals of good day care; staff requirements; children who need day care; day care for infants; family day care; after-school day care; industry-related day care; and family needs and educational goals. Bryant Fillion, in the final chapter of the book, discusses the way that schools influence children's language through instruction, the school environment, and processes of evaluation. He uses the principles of language development introduced in earlier chapters to assess schools as enabling or disabling environments.

PART I

THE NATURE OF LANGUAGE DEVELOPMENT

Chapter 1

The Negotiation of Meaning: Talking and Learning at Home and at School

Gordon Wells

Ontario Institute for Studies in Education

I was traveling on the train between Bristol and London on a recent visit to England and noticed a girl about 7 years old get into the compartment with her grandmother, who, to help pass the time, had brought some comics for the child to read. On the back of one of them was a game involving a track of small squares along which the players had to move their pieces according to the roll of dice. Needless to say, the girl soon announced that she wanted to play this game but, as her grandmother pointed out, they did not have a pair of dice. The child was obviously disappointed until, after a moment's thought, her grandmother suggested that they could perhaps still play if they could improvise with numbers written on paper. The child then took a piece of paper and, with some help, tore it into six pieces and carefully wrote the numbers 1 to 6 on them. They then devised a way of covering the pieces at random. Having agreed in this way on an alternative means of achieving the effect of rolling the dice, they proceeded happily to play the game.

I have described this anecdote in some detail because it seemed to me, as I looked on, to illustrate very clearly what I intended by the title of this chapter "The Negotiation of Meaning." What I had in mind was two or more people working together to resolve a problem by means of talking, thinking, and acting in collaboration.

Not every instance of language use is so obviously undertaken to solve a problem in the external world. But communication itself is inherently problematic and so collaboration is always required—an attempt by each to understand the intention of the other and to respond in terms of that understanding. Even an argument requires collaboration of a kind. As the saying goes: "It takes two to make a quarrel." So, although to claim that all language use involves collaboration may seem too obvious a point to be worth making, I still think it is worth pursuing further, for reasons that I hope will become apparent.

When people talk about conversation—of talking things over or of having a discussion—they often use expressions such as "exchanging ideas" or "conveying their meaning," or—more formally—of "bringing minds into contact." What seems to be implied by the use of such phrases is a belief that, by speaking, a person can cause a listener to come to have the same thoughts as were in his or her own mind at the time of speaking. But, as will become clear from a moment's reflection, this is altogether impossible.

Suppose I were to try to "share with you," the reader, some event in my life, for example my childhood memory of accompanying the local milk delivery man as he made his rounds in his horse-drawn cart, in which there were four or five large churns of milk. I used to sit on the back of the cart and, at each stop, I would climb down and fetch the pitcher that was standing on the back doorstep of the house and bring it to the cart to be filled from one of the churns with a huge ladle.

In reading this brief account, you will, I hope, have been able to construct a general idea of the experience and, if I added more detail, you might achieve a somewhat sharper impression. But try as I may, I shall never succeed in conveying its meaning for me. And I don't simply mean the feelings, as I recall them now: What a great adventure it was, as a 5-year-old, to spend the morning traveling down unfamiliar back streets in this way; and how seriously I took the responsibility of spotting the houses at which we had to call, fetching the pitchers and putting them safely back on the doorsteps without spilling a drop. Equally impossible to convey are the specific sense impressions I recall: the horse's breath steaming in the cold air, the unevenness of the cobbled streets, the gauze covers with colored glass beads that had to be put over the pitchers, and so on. With each additional detail, the picture may be becoming clearer, but it is still not the same as the picture that is in my mind.

There are three reasons for this. First, my ideas arise out of *my* experience, and that is unique to me, just as yours is to you. No two people have the same accumulation of specific experiences, and so no two people have identical ideas. Secondly, no two people have identical linquistic resources, and so the ways in which we use words and structures vary slightly from one person to another, even within the same linguistic community. Thirdly, the language code itself only corresponds in a very rough way to experience, since words refer to classes of objects, attributes and events, while experience is made up of specific instances, which are unique in their particularity. Furthermore, in speaking or writing, words have to follow each other one at a time, whereas experience is multifaceted and simultaneous.

So, when I try to "convey" my ideas to a listener or a reader, there are many steps at which the sharpness and precision of my personal thoughts and feelings become blurred, as I draw from the mental representation of my experience the salient aspects that I decide to communicate, and then select from my linguistic resources the items of vocabulary and grammatical structure that, in my judgment, will most adequately encode them, and finally articulate them in speech or writing. But, of course, all that is available to the receiver is a stream of sounds, with accompanying gestures and intonation, or a sequence of marks on the page, which, in themselves, have no meaning at all. For receivers to understand my meaning, a related process is required in which they construct an interpretation based on their own experiences, which they judge to match the decoded sequence of sounds or marks. In other words, as a receiver, one never knows what the sender means—what thoughts he or she is trying to communicate; one only knows what thoughts one would have had in mind if one had spoken or written the same sentences oneself.

Seen in this light, it is clear that communication *must* involve collaboration, and at a very fundamental level. For, if the sender wants the receiver to construct a meaning that is close to the one he has in mind, he must, as he selects and encodes his message, take account of the needs of the receiver and of the basis of knowledge and experience that the receiver will be able to draw on in forming his or her interpretation. Similarly, in performing that constructive act of interpretation, the receiver must try to imagine what meanings the sender is likely to be trying to communicate on this particular occasion. Fortunately, all does not depend on a single sentence. In conversation, particularly, the listener can ask for help in the form of requests for clarification or further information and, when he responds, the fit between the response and what has just been said allows the original speaker to judge how close the listener's interpretation is to what the speaker intended. Both with respect to individual utterances, therefore, and in the shared construction of longer sequences, meanings are negotiated as the conversation progresses.

Learning to Talk

If communication through language is such a complex and chancy business, one might well wonder how anyone ever learns to do it. And indeed it is a remarkable achievement. But over the last quarter of a century, as a result of an ever-increasing number of studies of various kinds, we are now rather closer to being able to explain, at least in broad outline, how it occurs.

Let us start with some incontrovertible facts. First, at birth the human infant knows no language at all. Indeed, the baby does not even know what a language is. Second, by the age of 2, all but the very small minority of children who are severely handicapped have begun to speak and understand the language of the community in which they are growing up, and by 5 they have more or less achieved a basic mastery of it. Third, despite very substantial differences between children in both the quality and the quantity of their experience of language in use, for any particular language (or dialect of a language), the order in which the items within the various subsystems of the language are acquired is very similar indeed from one child to another. At the same time, it is very clear that children do not all develop at the same rate, nor do they all use the resources they have acquired in exactly the same ways or for exactly the same purposes. (For detailed accounts see Brown, 1973; Crystal, Fletcher, & Garman, 1976; Wells, 1985.) There are thus both strong similarities between children but also some recognizable differences, both of which will need to be taken into account when they start going to school.

In trying to account for these facts, and in particular for the strong similarities between children in the sequence in which their learning takes place and for the substantial differences in their rate of learning, we shall need to look more closely at the two essential components: what each child brings to the task by way of biological endowment (nature) and the conversations that he or she experiences, particularly those in which he or she participates (nurture). As with all other aspects of human development, the processes and outcomes of learning are a result of an interaction between these two components.

Until quite recently, it was thought that nurture was the more important. According to Skinner (1957), for example, (and other behaviorist psychologists), the acquisition of language was seen to be the result of a form of conditioning—a progressive shaping of the infant's spontaneous vocal behavior by means of positive and negative reinforcement on the part of the parents and other caretakers until the language "habits" of the community had been built up and become firmly established. However, the factual inaccuracy of this account was clearly established by the pioneering observational work of Roger Brown and his colleagues (1969) in the 1960s and its theoretical impossibility conclusively demonstrated by George Miller (1965) at about the same time.

Both these lines of attack owed much to the theoretical work of Noam Chomsky (1965), who set out to explain how speakers of a language have essentially the same knowledge of the "rules" which underlie the indefinitely large numbers of grammatically well-formed sentences that can be spoken and understood. Chomsky's claim, revolutionary at the time, was that every human infant is equipped with a language acquisition device—a biologically based predisposition to construct a representation of the language of his or her community according to certain universal principles. In effect, what Chomsky was doing was arguing for the pre-eminence, in language learning, of the other essential component—that of nature.

What made Chomsky's claim so revolutionary was the still prevailing view of the human baby as essentially passive, waiting to be intellectually (and linguistically) molded by the impact of the environment. Although that view was challenged long ago by Piaget, it is only in the last 20 years or so that work with children in the first year of life has been able to demonstrate just how mistaken it was. In the present context, there are two particular aspects that I want to describe in some detail for, together, they provide the basis for the launch into language.

The first is the predisposition to make sense of experience. It is said that nature abhors a vacuum, and similarly we could say about human beings that they abhor "no-sense." Faced with incoming information received through the senses, we have an urge, a built-in drive beyond our conscious control, to construct a story within which the separate bits of information will make sense. Richard Gregory (1974) refers to such stories as "brain fictions" and he argues that they are the essential building blocks of our mental model of the world, allowing us to recognize objects and events, predict possible outcomes, and plan our actions so that we can achieve our personal goals.

This active meaning-making is already observable in the first weeks of life. For example, in one experiment, Tom Bower (1974) had babies watch a face-like shape that moved in an arc through their field of vision on the end of a long bar. Having ascertained that they could track the moving object, Bower introduced a large screen behind which the object disappeared after traversing a small portion of the arc. Reliably, the babies moved their gaze so that they were ready to pick up the object when it re-emerged from behind the screen. What this tells us is that such young infants not only have a rudimentary concept of an object continuing to exist even when temporarily obscured from view, but also that they are able to use information about trajectory and velocity to predict when and where the moving object will reappear.

What this experiment and others like it show is that infants do not have to wait to be taught in order to come to know. From the beginning, they are active agents in constructing an internal model of the world with which they interact, a model which becomes progressively broader in scope and more effective in integrating information from both internal and external sources.

The second characteristic that is essential for language learning is the infant's predisposition to initiate interactions with other people. From careful observations recorded on film by researchers such as Colwyn Trevarthen (1979) and Daniel Stern (1977), we can see how the baby's gestures, such as pursing the lips, raising an eyebrow, or stretching out a hand, call forth a response from the mother, leading to quite long chains of exchanges which have all the appearance of "conversations without words." Initially, the success of these exchanges is dependent on the mother's fitting her responses to the baby's initiations and, even as the baby grows into childhood, it remains important that her behavior be contingently responsive.

Recently I visited a friend whose first baby had been born just 2 days previously. The baby could already raise her head off the pillow and move it around; but what was even more interesting was the new mother's behavior. When she picked her baby up, she scanned her face for expressions of meaning, interpreting even the slightest gesture, such as a fleeting smile, as intended to communicate, and responding with an answering smile or words of appreciation. Like all other parents, she was treating her baby as if she were already human—as if she were capable of experiencing differentiated mental states and of having intentions to communicate them. And so, as Newson puts it (1978), by being treated as if they already had recognizable intentions and responded to accordingly, babies do indeed come to have the intentions that are appropriate within the culture to which they belong.

With a drive to interact with others and a developing mental model which enables the infant to make sense of the shared environment, the stage is set for the emergence of language. The first step is the establishment of "intersubjectivity" in those interactions described by Trevarthen, the state in which both participants know that both know that they are attending to each other. In such episodes of joint attention, the infant is able to discover that the vocal noises that his or her partner makes are in some way significant. The next task is to find out how.

Put in very general terms, what the infant has to do is construct a theory with two related parts. The first part is concerned with the substance of language: recognizing similarities and differences between the utterances that he or she hears and working out the systems in terms of which words, phrases, and sentences are constructed. The second part is concerned with the way in which recognizable sequences of sound are related to the situations in which they occur, that is to say with the meanings that they are intended to convey.

Now as we have already seen in the first part of this chapter, in order to discover what somebody else means by what they say, we have to construct a matching utterance and decide what we ourselves would mean—what state of affairs we should be referring to and what we should want our partner to do or think about it—if we were to produce it in the same situation. And this in essence is what language learners have to do. But, simultaneously, they also have to use the same information as a basis for hypothesizing about the relationship between meaning and sound and about the organization of the language system. In effect, what they have to do, therefore, is to reinvent language; and, what is more, they have to perform this formidably difficult task for themselves. For, precisely because infants do not yet have a language, they are unable to benefit from efforts by their parents to teach them, since they cannot understand their utterances, even if the parents themselves are able themselves to explain how language works.

To emphasize the extent to which the child must be the constructor of his or her own knowledge, however, is not to deny the contribution of the people in the child's environment. What the learner needs in order to carry out this task is evidence, which is what the parents and other members of the community provide when they talk to the child about the situations in which they are jointly engaged. What is more, they tend to make a variety of adjustments in their own behavior in order to make that evidence more easily accessible. Jerome Bruner, who has carried out very detailed studies of this stage of language development (1983), points to a variety of "formats," as he calls them, in which highly patterned routines, such as playing peekaboo or exchanging objects or, later, looking at a picture book, are repeated almost verbatim, with the adult initially playing both roles and then gradually withdrawing the support as the child shows ability to take over one of the roles.

Adults certainly can make the language-learning task easier for the child, by providing this sort of "scaffolding." But not all adults adopt these strategies to the same extent and, in some cultures, it appears, they hardly make any concessions to the immaturity of the child. Yet even under these conditions, children eventually become competent speakers of their community's language. On the other hand, when adults do adopt strategies that make it easier for their children to participate in conversation, the children not only tend to talk more, but to develop more rapidly.

From a comparison of the various studies in which potentially facilitating features of adult speech have been investigated, I think four principles can be extracted that should guide the adult conversationalist:

1. Take the child's attempts to initiate conversation seriously by listening with interest to what he or she has to say.
2. Because the child's utterances are often incomplete, ambiguous, or in other ways difficult to understand, take pains to make sure you

have correctly interpreted his or her intended meaning.

3. In responding, make the child's meaning the point of departure for your contribution; your words are then more likely to match his or her understanding of the situation and so to provide useful evidence for theory building and testing.
4. In deciding what to say and in selecting the form in which to say it, take account of the child's ability to comprehend. This does not mean staying always within the child's current range, for that would be to deprive him or her of opportunities for growth. But it does mean constantly monitoring the child's comprehension and adopting appropriate strategies to simplify or repair when problems occur.

Evidence from the Bristol Study

In the preceding section I have discussed mainly the first year or year and a half of life. Until quite recently it was thought that language development did not really begin until some point well into the second year, when the child begins to put words together in some form of grammatical structure. What I have tried to show, though, is that language emerges naturally out of earlier forms of cognitive and social behavior, which provide a necessary foundation. In a very important sense, then, language development starts at birth, with the baby's first interactions with the social and physical environment. It is true, however, that recognizable use of the conventional forms of the adult language only begins to appear during the second year. And so it is at that point that we can see most clearly how adherence by an adult to the principles just enumerated can facilitate the child's progressive mastery of the language system.

In the Bristol study we followed the language development of a representative sample of 128 children from 15 to 60 months, recording each child's spontaneous conversation at intervals over a complete day, once ever 3 months. In this way, we were not only able to chart the children's sequence of language development but also to study their conversational experience in order to identify the features of adult behavior that are associated with accelerated development. In the previous section, I drew heavily on the results of this investigation. (For a detailed account, see Wells, 1985.) Now I want to illustrate some of the claims made above by considering a number of particular examples.

The first extract comes from a recording made of Mark shortly after his second birthday. At this age, he was producing quite a range of utterances in which words were combined, so that he was able both to identify the topic of interest and make some comment about it. However, he had not yet mastered the use of the inversion of subject and auxiliary verb to ask questions (e.g., "Do you . . . ?" "Is it . . . ?"), so he used a rising intonation contour instead. In the present instance, Mark is standing by a central heating radiator. He can feel the heat coming from it and he wants to bring this interesting experience to his mother's attention. From the rising intonation, we might also surmise that he is simultaneously asking his mother to confirm the appropriateness of this way of referring to the experience.

1. Mark: *Hot, Mummy?*
2. Mother: *Hot? Yes, that's the radiator.*
3. Mark: *Been—burn?*
4. Mother: *Burn?*
5. Mark: *Yeah.*
6. Mother: *Yes, you know it'll burn, don't you.*
7. Mark: [*putting hand on radiator*] *Oh! Oh!*
8. Mother: *Take your hand off of it.*
9. Mark: *Uh?*
10. Mother: [*asking if he needs his other shoelace tied*]: *What about the other shoe?*
11. Mark: *It all done, Mummy.*
12. Mother: *Mm?*
13. Mark: *It done, Mummy.*
14. Mother: *It's done, is it?*
15. Mark: *Yeah.*
16. Mother: *Oh.*

[*Mark tries to get up to see out of the window*]

17. *No! Leave the curtain.*
18. Mark: *Oh, up please.*
19. Mother: *Leave the curtain, please.*
20. Mark: *No.*
21. Mother: *Leave the curtain, Mark.*
22. Mark: *No*

[*Looking out of window, he sees a man digging in his garden*]

23. *A man—a man er—dig—down there.*
24. Mother: *A man walked down there?*
25. Mark: *Yeah.*
26. Mother: *Oh, yes.*
27. Mark: *Oh, yes.*

[*6-second pause*]

28. *A man's fire. Mummy.*
29. Mother: *Mm?*
30. Mark: *A man's fire.*

31. Mother: *Mummy's flower?*
32. Mark: *No.*
33. Mother: *What?*
34. Mark: [*emphasizing each word*] *Mummy, the man, fire.*
35. Mother: *Man's fire?*
36. Mark: *Yeah.*
37. Mother: *Oh, yes, the bonfire.*
38. Mark: [*imitating*] *Bonfire.*
39. Mother: *Mm.*
40. Mark: *Bonfire. Oh, bonfire. Bonfire. Bon—a fire bo—bonfire.*
41. *Oh, hot, Mummy. Oh, hot. It hot. It hot.*
42. Mother: *Mm. It will burn, won't it?*
43. Mark: *Yeah. Burn. It burn.*

To understand what is happening here, it is helpful to think of any conversation as establishing and developing a triangle of communication, in which the three points represent, at any stage, the speaker, the listener, and the topic of joint attention.

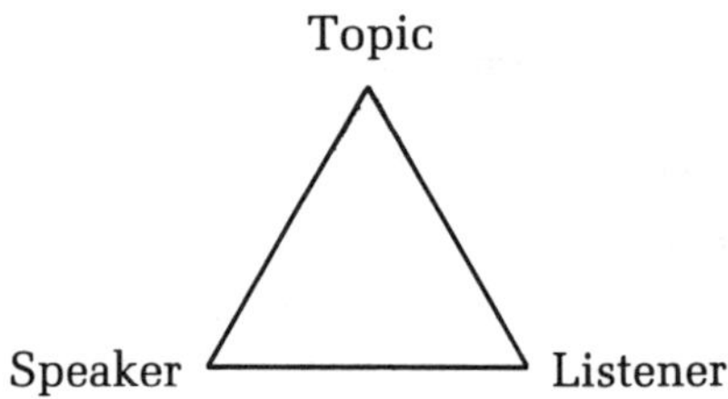

In the early interactions studied by Trevarthen, attention was focused almost exclusively on the speaker–listener axis—on the establishment of intersubjectivity. By the end of the first year, as both Trevarthen and Bruner have shown, adult and child are able to build on this interpersonal axis to make an object the focus or topic of joint attention, thereby completing the triangle of communication at a preverbal level. One way of thinking of the development of communication during the second year, then, is as a recapitulation of this construction of the triangle, but now using verbal means.

By the stage Mark has reached in this example, gaining an adult's attention and indicating the topic for joint attention can be attempted in the same utterance. So Mark's first utterance both calls for mother's attention and makes a comment about the topic (the radiator), which he takes for granted. Intuitively following the conversational principles outlined above, Mark's mother gives him her attention and checks to make sure that she has correctly understood what he has said. As Mark does not disagree, she continues by confirming the accuracy of his observation and then adds something to it—the name of the object that is causing his sensation and that is the focus of their joint attention. So now we have "hot" contributed by Mark and "the radiator" contributed by the mother, together yielding a more complex meaning: "The radiator [is] hot." Mark then develops this further by introducing "burn," again said with a questioning intonation. Once again mother checks that she has understood and, when this is confirmed, she confirms the appropriateness of the connection he has made. Then—and this is what is so fascinating about this short extract—she reflects the whole, jointly constructed, proposition back to Mark, bringing it to the level of his conscious awareness: "You *know* it'll burn, don't you?"

Later in the extract (lines 23–27), we have a good example of what happens when the adult fails to understand the child's meaning: The conversation just peters out in mutual incomprehension. But a moment later, on the subject of the man's fire, Mark is not willing to give up so easily (lines 28–39). In order to make his meaning clear, he enunciates his words more clearly, leaving a pause between them (and thereby, incidentally, demonstrating his ability to segment consciously the stream of speech into words). Mother now understands and responds by supplying the name of this particular type of fire ("bonfire"). For Mark, this information comes at just the right moment. He is looking at the bonfire, thinking about it, and he is really interested in it. Hearing the word in this context, he learns it instantly and will probably never forget it.

Finally, the conversation returns to the topic with which it started: "fire–hot–burn" (lines 41–43). One could describe this as an almost perfect language-learning lesson—except, of course, that the mother had no prearranged lesson plan, no predetermined curricular sequence in which this was a discrete step. Instead, she quite spontaneously responded to the child's interest and, having checked that she had correctly understood his meaning, extended it in terms that she judged would be appropriate to his level of comprehension. This is what I had in mind when talking earlier about "the negotiation and development of meaning."

My second example involves a different mother–child pair. James is 3½ years old. In this extract, he has just been playing in the garden and, as he enters the house, his mother helps him to change out of his muddy clothes.

Mother: *There we are [mother helping James to change).*
There—one slipper on.

James: *I can see a bird.*

Mother: *A what, love?*

James: *[James watching bird in garden]*

James: *See a bird.*

Mother: *Is there? Outside? [whispers]*

James: *Yes [whispers].*

James: *See [whispers pointing to bird].*

Mother: *Is he eating anything? [whispers]*

James: *No [whispers].*

Mother: *Where? [whispers throughout].*
Oh yes he's getting . . .
Do you know what he's doing?

James: *No [whispers].*

Mother: *He's going to the . . . the . . . paper sack to try and pick out some pieces—Oh he's got some food there*
And I expect he'll pick out some pieces of thread from the sack to go and make his nest . . . up . . . underneath the roof,
James, wait a minute and I'll . . .
OK wait a mo—wait a mo James.

James: *That bird's gone [whispers].*

Mother: *Has it gone now?*

James: *Yes [whispers].*

Mother: *Oh.*
Take those long trousers off because they're . . . a bit muddy in there.

In comparison with Mark at the age of 2, one can readily see that there has been a considerable development of competence, particularly in the management of conversation. There are in fact two quite different conversational topics here: The first, which begins and ends the extract, is introduced by the mother and concerns getting clothes changed; the second is introduced by James and concerns the activities of the bird. About the first topic, the mother's intentions are perfectly clear; her concluding remark shows that there is going to be no negotiation about that. However, she is prepared temporarily to drop her topic in response to James's announced interest in the bird and, like Mark's mother, she observes the four principles that I suggested earlier in the way she responds. To begin with, she asks questions to make sure that she shares his focus of attention and, in so doing, she also helps him to sustain the conversation. Then, once she is sure the triangle of communication is established, she offers extending information about the shared topic: the bird and its activities. In this instance, the information she offers and the language in which it is expressed is probably right at the limit of James's ability to comprehend, but, because it is a topic he is interested in, he seems able at least to get the gist of it. So he is simultaneously being provided with evidence for learning language and evidence, in language, for extending his internal model of the world.

What I wish to claim is that conversations such as these—and our recordings contain quite a number—represent the best kind of preschool "curriculum," observed in action. Talking and learning occur simultaneously and spontaneously. Now it may indeed be an important characteristic of such conversations that the topics are typically initiated by the child (when the child initiates, it is almost certain that the topic is one that he or she is interested in), but it takes two to make conversation work: two to negotiate meaning and create the opportunity for learning to take place. And as I have tried to show, if one of the participants is relatively immature, a much greater responsibility falls on the other to make the most of the opportunities that occur and to create situations in which they are likely to arise. Not that this requires unusual skills or special training. (Neither of the mothers in the extracts quoted was highly educated.) The adult must, however, be genuinely interested in the child and, as a result, in the topics that he or she proposes, sensitive in understanding his or her intentions, and willing to take time to develop these topics and intentions through further talk. Although not difficult, the adult's role is crucial if the child is effectively to develop the ability to learn through language.

Linguistic Interaction in the Classroom

If these are the conditions that facilitate learning at home, we need to ask next how far these conditions also obtain at school. As far as the children are concerned, there is no reason to suppose that the strategies of active meaning-making they have used to good effect at home cannot continue to be equally effective in the classroom. But do they get the opportunity to use them?

Obviously, schools cannot simply provide a continuation of the home environment. First, even under the most generous staffing conditions, the teacher has responsibility for providing appropriate learning experiences for a much greater number of children. Secondly, as a corollary, it is at school that many children first find themselves having to get along with a large group of peers. So there are also important social skills to be learned. Thirdly, there is the curriculum. As representatives of the larger community, teachers have a responsibility to ensure that all children encounter those areas of knowledge, those skills and those values that society considers important. So there must be long-term goals concerning what it is hoped children will learn.

All these characteristics of schools will certainly mean that the classroom must be differently organized from the home. In particular, there will clearly be fewer opportunities for individual children to talk to the teacher just when they want to. But, in principle, there is no reason why, when there is a chance for interaction, it cannot have some of the facilitative characteristics that are found at home. Nevertheless, from our observations, this is all too rarely the case.

In a follow-up study of 32 children, we made a direct comparison of the language of the home and the language of the classroom, based on eight 5-minute samples recorded at intervals throughout a morning. All adult–children interaction was coded in terms of the function, content and form of each utterance and with respect to the relationship between child and adult utterances (for fuller accounts, see Wells, 1986a, 1986b). The results of the comparison showed that:

- Whereas children address fewer utterances to teachers than to adults at home, an almost equal number is addressed to the children in each of the two settings;
- At school, children initiate less than a quarter of conversations with their teachers, while at home they initiate almost two thirds of all conversations with adults;
- Children's utterances to teachers are both syntactically less complex than those they address to their parents and they also draw on a narrower, less complex range of meanings;
- At school, children ask less than one-fifth of the number of questions that they ask at home; they make far fewer references to non-present events and produce a much higher proportion of incomplete and fragmentary utterances (this being the result of the much higher proportion of teacher questions that require only a single word or phrase as an answer);
- Teachers are only half as likely as parents to extend the meanings that children offer; by contrast, they are more than twice as likely as parents to ignore the child's meaning and to continue to develop the topic about which they were previously talking.

Underlying all these specific comparisons is the general tendency of teachers to dominate conversation in the classroom, insisting that their topics and their criteria of relevance are the ones that will hold sway.

It is not surprising, therefore, that many children adopt a passive role, only speaking when they are spoken to and offering the minimum by way of contribution. It is this nonreciprocal style of interaction that leads to a substantial number of children's being perceived and labeled as "linguistically deficient" or even "nonverbal" by their teachers. And these descriptions then all too easily become self-fulfilling prophecies.

Consider the following extract from a typical interaction between Rosie and her teacher. On this occasion the teacher is showing a multi-ethnic group some slides of India. She has put a slide into the viewer and asks Rosie to describe what she can see. What she wants Rosie to mention is an animal that is in the background of the picture, but that is not what Rosie wants to talk about.

Teacher: *They're Indian ladies and what else?*

Rosie: *I can see something*

Teacher: *What can you see?*

Rosie: *And they're going into the sand*

Teacher: *Mm? [Teacher does not follow Rosie's meaning]*

Rosie: *You have a look [Rosie hands back the viewer]*

Teacher: *Well you have a look and tell me*
[Hands viewer back to Rosie]
I've seen it already
I want to see if you can see
[6 seconds pause while Rosie looks]

Rosie: *Oh they're going in the sand*
[20 seconds pause but Teacher does not hear these comments as she is busy with other children]

Teacher: *What's behind the men?*
Can you see the men in the red coats?
[2 seconds pause while Rosie still looks]
Can you see the men in the red coats?
What is behind . . . those men?
[4 seconds pause]

Rosie: *[Rosie nods]*

Teacher: *What is it?*

Rosie: *They're walking in—*

Teacher: *Pardon?*

Rosie: *They're walking*

Teacher: *They're walking, yes*
But what's walking behind them?
Something very big

Rosie: *A horse*

Teacher: *It's much bigger than a horse*
It's much bigger than a horse
It's big and gray and it's got a long nose that we call a trunk

Rosie: *Trunk [repeating]*

Teacher: *Can you see what it is?*
What is it?

Rosie: *[Rosie nods]*
[another child mutters something inaudible]

Teacher: *No, that's what his nose is*
Can you see what the animal is?

Rosie: *No [meaning I can't guess]*

Teacher: *It's much bigger than a horse*
Let's give it to Darren and see if Darren knows
[20 second pause while Darren looks. Rosie puts her thumb in her mouth. Teacher looks for more pictures in books.]

Teacher: *There's a picture of the animal that was walking behind the men—with the red coats on.*
What's that? [Teacher shows picture to Rosie]

Rosie: *The soldiers*

Teacher: *Mm?*

Rosie: *Soldiers*

Darren: *Elephant*

Teacher: *What's that?*
[Teacher points to the elephant]

Rosie: *An elephant*

The complete episode takes about 5 minutes and, despite a variety of prompts from the teacher, Rosie consistently adopts strategies that the teacher judges inappropriate for the task as she has presented it. Rosie persists in describing only the people she can see in the picture and either does not see the elephant or, if she does, does not understand the teacher's intention that she should name it or admit her ignorance of the name and ask for the teacher's help.

This is perhaps a somewhat extreme example, but we observed many interactions in which children who were well able, like Rosie, to hold interesting conversations at home were rendered incompetent by teachers who were either unable or unwilling to adopt a reciprocal style of interaction, in which the child's meanings and intentions were treated as worthy of interested attention. In short, just as much as at home, therefore, it is incumbent on the more mature partner in the interaction to be contingently responsive to the child's expression of interest in, and understanding of, a topic, if the child is to be enabled to learn through conversation.

Empowering Teachers to Negotiate the Curriculum

Since so many teachers are themselves parents of young children, we can reasonably ask why, in school, they fail to behave according to the principles that they observe, quite intuitively, at home—principles, moreover, that they probably agree should apply equally to adult–child interaction in the classroom. The answer, I believe, must lie in the inappropriate model that they have constructed of what it is to be a teacher, on the basis of their own experiences as students, and from their training as teachers. According to this model, teaching is essentially a matter of transmitting predetermined packages of knowledge or skill to children and then testing to ensure that the same material can be reproduced by the children, preferably in exactly the same form as that in which it was transmitted.

However, as was explained in the first section of this chapter, this model of teaching is based on a totally false view of linguistic communication. Listeners can only construct an interpretation of the speaker's meaning on the basis of their own current understanding of the topic, and that depends on the mental model they have constructed on the basis of their own previous experience. When this model is, relatively speaking, immature (as will nearly always be the case where young children are concerned), the meaning that the child constructs will inevitably be different from that which is in the mind of the teacher (who has had the benefit of up to 20 years of education). With no opportunity for the negotiation of meaning, it is hardly surprising that children so often fail to learn what is expected of them.

The underlying problem with this "transmission" model of teaching is that children tend to be treated as relatively passive recipients of information, expected to listen quietly while the teacher talks and then to complete ditto sheets and other routine exercises. Thus they are deprived of opportunities actively to construct their own knowledge and, in many cases, actually discouraged from employing those strategies for making sense that they employ to good effect at home and in other settings outside the classroom.

Why, then, do teachers continue to adopt an approach which, if they reflected on their own experience as learners and as parents, they would recognize to be inappropriate? A part of the answer can be found, I believe, in the metaphors that are nowadays all too frequently used for talking about education—metaphors that seem to be drawn from the world of industrial management in a mass-production economy. Use of terms such as "plant," "input output," "cost-effectiveness" and so on betrays a conception of education as a factory assembly line. I even heard two educators recently talking about "tooling up the curriculum" for the coming school year! Such metaphors suggest a belief that, as in a factory, if one sets up the curriculum as a production line with the right machines in the right sequence, with teachers as machine operators and quality controllers, then the raw material (children) which goes in at one end will emerge at the other as acceptable, identical products.

Stated in these terms, this is clearly not a philosophy to which any teachers I know would happily subscribe. Yet more and more it seems to be dominating actual practice. On the other hand, there are classrooms and, indeed, whole schools in which teachers have found ways of enabling children to engage actively in meaning-making, building cumulatively on what they know and can do, and learning through collaboration with their peers as well as with their teachers. The following extract comes from such a classroom, in which a small group of children were looking with their teachers at a collection of twigs, which had been gathered on the nearby common.[1]

Yelshea: *Miss, why has—why has it gone all furry? Most plants that I see—wild plants—are not furry.*
But is there anything that's meant to—why it's meant to be furry?

Teacher: *What do you other children—[to Richard]—what do you think?*

Richard: *'Cos, er—it—protects it.*

Colin: *It's a warm coat . . . that keeps it warm if it opens up too early.*

Yelshea: *It could be, because I can see the green—little bit of green inside and—I see green there . . . sort of protecting it.*

Donna: *Like my plant—*

Teacher: *I beg your pardon?*

Donna: *It's like my plant. Mine's all furry.*

Teacher: *Which plant is this?*

---

[1] I am grateful to Moira McKenzie, Warden of the Center for Language in Primary Education, Inner London Education Authority, for permission to reprint this extract.

Donna: *I don't know which—which one I've planted, though. Might be the oak one.*

Teacher: *Why do you think that needs protecting?*

Colin: *Protecting from the cold so's it doesn't die.*

Yelshea: *No, or protecting from the sticky bud. It might get up and stick all around it.*

Teacher: *Do you know how we—how we could find out about why it needs protecting?*

Yelshea: *I know. Just watch it.*

Richard: *From a book.*

Colin: *Just study and . . . find out.*

Teacher: *Which book would you look in, Richard?*

Richard: *[turning to get one from the shelf] I'd look in, um, this book.*

Teacher: *Yes. It's not over there. I know which one you mean.*

Richard: *That big book* ['Trees and leaves'].

Teacher: *This one?*

Richard: *Yes.*

Teacher: *You have a little look through that while Nicola says what she was going to say.*

Nicola: *Miss, you know this bit here? It looks like—You know them sweet lollies and things?*
Well it looks like that. And this bit here, it's different from the other bit. Or is it another plant?
[She fingers the leaf of the horse chestnut.] Because look.

Teacher: *Bring it closer to yourself.*

Colin: *I think it's the same—it's the same plant, except the sticky bud is still underneath it . . . if you can see it. All round this side. You can see it, can't you?*
[The teacher speaks to another child who has just entered the room.]

Richard: *[indicating a picture in the book] Is this the sticky bud? Is this the one? This one here?*

Teacher: *Hang on. [Taking book] Can I show you this book, which Richard's seen before?*

Colin: *[reading]* 'Trees and leaves.'

Yelshea: *Trees and leaves.*

Richard: *Miss, was that it what I just showed you—sticky bud?*

Teacher: *Yes, I know that you've looked in this book.*
I saw you looking the other day.

Donna: *****[inaudible]*

Colin: *Is it—is it wild? Is it a wild book or just a plain book that you usually see?*

Teacher: *What do you mean?*

Yelshea: *Sort of . . . like wild plants . . . and stuff like in the common.*

Colin: *Does it have just normal everyday trees, or does it have great big wild trees?*

Teacher: *[handing book to Colin] Well, would you like to see?*

Yelshea: *Um, would it, um, be like the things in the common there?*
If they found out about that and wild things and all things that grow in different places.

Nicole: *Miss, those * look like—*

Teacher: *Do you know where you'd look in the book to find out whether it tells you about trees that you'd find on the common? Where—where would you look in the book?*

Donna: *On the tree page.*

Yelshea: *Miss . . . the wildlife, wildlife.*

Teacher: *Shall I show you? If you look in this book with Richard.*

Colin: *That's got the contents.*

Teacher: *Yes. Right in the front it's got what's called the "contents."*

Colin: *Which has got a list of everything that's in it. It's got little pages or little—or a few pages about whatever it says, like—[Several children speak at the same time].*

Donna: *The fruit ones.*

Colin: *[reading] "What to look for on a tree." That's one.*

Teacher: *If you wanted to find out about these horse chestnuts, Nicola, what would you look for in the Contents? What would you look for? [She passes the book to Nicola.] Have a little read through it and see if you can find the part that will help you.*

What is striking about this extract is the willingness of the children to say what they think, offering observations and opinions and trying out hypotheses without fear of being wrong. As a result, the teacher is able to gain some important insights into how much the children understand and to tailor her contributions accordingly. At the same time, she clearly has her own intention, which is to introduce the use of reference books as a means of complementing and informing direct observation. However, she is able to introduce the use of these particular books as a natural extension of the children's existing interest in finding out about the twigs. In this context, learning how to use a contents page has an evident purpose, which the children understand and enthusiastically attempt to make their own.

For children to have this active involvement in their own learning, however, it is necessary to find ways of enabling them to share in the responsibility for deciding what tasks to undertake, planning the procedures to be used and evaluating the outcomes. In short, what is required is a curriculum that is emergent and negotiated, rather than predetermined and teacher-directed.

This, in turn, requires teachers to be given greater responsibility for what happens in their own classrooms, and resources and support to enable them to take on their responsibility with confidence. Clearly, teacher educators, principals, and school board personnel have an important role to play in this respect and, for some of them, it will call for a radical rethinking of their current beliefs and practices. It may be overoptimistic, therefore, to expect changes at this level to happen quickly. However, whether this administrative support is forthcoming or not, there is a great deal that individual teachers can do to change their own working patterns, thereby improving the opportunities for learning of the children for whom they are responsible.

First they can try, in their conversations with individual children, more frequently to adopt a negotiatory style of interaction, by listening more carefully to what the child has to say, allowing him or her longer to think before jumping in with the correct answer or a further question and, most importantly, taking the child's meaning as the basis for their own next contribution. Like adults, children rarely talk nonsense. Although their answers and opinions may be erroneous from an adult point of view, they represent the best sense the children can make of the issue or problem at hand at this stage in their individual development. Children's utterances thus provide the most valid point of departure for the teacher's intervention, enabling him or her to help the children to reflect on what they know, on the strategies they are using, and on possible sources of evidence relevant to the task in which they are engaged.

Secondly, teachers can see their classrooms as places in which they too can learn. By listening to what their children say and by observing them at work, teachers can increase their general understanding of how children learn and, specifically what each individual child already knows and can do. They can thus make more informed choices about what sort of learning opportunities to provide—about the topics and activities that are most likely to enable the children to develop from where they are now in directions that lead to those long-term goals to which the teacher is committed.

Self-observation can also be a source of learning. For example, one can record oneself when talking with individuals or groups. Alternatively, teachers can team up with colleagues to observe each other. Often we are unaware how much our practice differs from our intentions, so we need the sort of objective information that is obtained from recording, or systematic observation, in order to evaluate ourselves and provide a basis for planning change, if that seems to be called for.

Finally, teachers are not alone. By sharing their observations with their colleagues and by discussing changes they plan to make or the results of those they have already made, they can learn from each other and, at the same time, provide that mutual support and encouragement that enables individuals to take risks as they try new ways of working.

In these ways, then, every teacher can do much to turn his or her school and classroom into an environment in which everyone is actively engaged in constructing knowledge through the collaborative use of language in which meanings are negotiated and extended.

References

Bower, T. (1974). *Development in infancy*. San Francisco: W. H. Freeman.

Brown, R. A. (1973). *A first language*. Cambridge, MA: Harvard University Press.

Brown, R., Cazden, C. & Bellugi, U. (1969). The child's grammar from I to III. In J. P. Hill (Ed.), *The 1967 Minnesota Symposium on Child Psychology*. (Vol. 2). Minneapolis: University of Minnesota Press.

Bruner, J. S. (1983). *Child's talk*. New York: Norton.

Chomsky, N. (1965). *Aspects of the theory of syntax*. Cambridge, MA: MIT Press.

Crystal, D., Fletcher, P, & Garman M. (1976). *The grammatical analysis of language disability*. London: Edward Arnold.

Gregory, R. (May, 1974). Psychology: Towards a science of fiction. *New Society, 23*, 439–441.

Miller, G. A. (1965). Some preliminaries to psycholinguistics. *American Psychologist, 20*, 15–20.

Newson, J. (1978). Dialogue and development. In A. Lock (Ed.), *Action, gesture and symbol: The emergence of language*. New York: Academic Press.

Skinner, B. F. (1957). *Verbal behavior*. New York: Appleton-Century-Crofts.

Stern, D. (1977). *The first relationship: Infant and mother*. London: Open Books.

Trevarthen, C. (1979). Communication and cooperation in early infancy. In M. Bullowa (Ed.), *Before speech: The beginnings of interpersonal communication*. Cambridge: Cambridge University Press.

Wells, G. (1985). *Language development in the pre-school years*. Cambridge: Cambridge University Press.

Wells, G. (1986). The language experience of five-year-old children at home and at school. In J. Cook-Gumperz (Ed.), *Literacy, language and schooling*. Cambridge: Cambridge University Press.

Wells, G. (1986). *The meaning makers*. Portsmouth, NH: Heinemann Educational Books.

Chapter 2

The Learning of Literacy

Gordon Wells

Ontario Institute for Studies in Education

In the previous chapter, I concentrated on the development of conversation, describing how children acquire their first language and simultaneously use that language to learn about the world around them. From the evidence reviewed, I concluded that these two related processes are learner-driven and learner-paced; that is, they are dependent on the children's active predisposition to make sense of their experience and to construct progressively more complex representations of what they know in order to be able to act more effectively in the world as they encounter it. At the same time, I emphasized the important role of the adults in the children's environment, both in providing the evidence from which they construct their representations and in motivating and facilitating these meaning-making processes. In sum, while emphasizing the active role of the child in his or her own learning, I also stressed the interactional nature of this learning, and hence the potentially significant contribution of the child's parents, caretakers, and teachers.

In this chapter, I shall be concerned with the acquisition of literacy, and I shall argue that, in many respects, the same principles apply as in the acquisition of spoken language. At the same time, it is important to recognize that the typical conditions under which literacy is acquired are somewhat different: Whereas very few parents give systematic instruction with respect to spoken language, the vast majority of children growing up in literate societies attend schools in which systematic instruction in literacy is one of the major emphases of the curriculum. Our ultimate concern in this chapter, therefore, will be to consider what sort of instruction is best suited to the needs of the literacy learner.

Much of the information on which the previous chapter was based was drawn from a longitudinal study of a representative sample of 128 children who were regularly recorded in their homes between the ages of 15 and 60 months. In the first part of this chapter, I shall discuss a continuation of this study in which 32 of these children were followed to the end of their elementary education.[1] During these years, in addition to the observations made in their homes and classrooms, a variety of tests were administered to the children at 5, 7, and 10¼ years and, at the same ages, assessments were made of them by their teachers. Interviews were also carried out with their parents, their teachers and the school principals; finally, interviews were carried out with the children themselves during the last round of assessments.[2] The aim of this follow-up study was to try to account for differences between the children in their educational achievement. The question we asked was: What was it about these children's earlier experiences that could best explain the substantial differences between them in their educational achievement by the end of their elementary schooling? The answer, as will be seen, was very strongly related to their developing understanding and control of the processes of literacy.

Achievement at the End of the Elementary Years

The technique we employed was one of retrospective analysis. That is to say, we started from the vantage point of the end of the elementary stage of education and tried to discover which of the variables measured at earlier points in the children's development provided the best explanation for the differences in their subsequent achievement. The results of this analysis are presented in summary form in Figure 1.

Our first task was to obtain one overall measure of achievement at the end of the elementary years. To this end, we carried out a factor analysis on the scores from the various instruments we had administered: tests of reading and mathematics, tasks involving spoken and written production and the comprehensive assessment schedule which we had asked the teachers to complete for each child. From the results of this analysis a composite measure was derived, based on the following scores: reading, writing, vocabulary size, mathematics, and teacher assessment of study skills. This measure we labeled "overall achievement."

---

[1] This latter part of the Bristol Study, "Language at Home and at School," was supported by grants from the Spencer Foundation and from the Department of Education and Science, for whose generosity I wish to express my appreciation.

[2] For a more detailed account of this whole longitudinal study, see G. Wells, (1986). *The meaning makers*. Portsmouth, NH: Heinemann Educational Books.

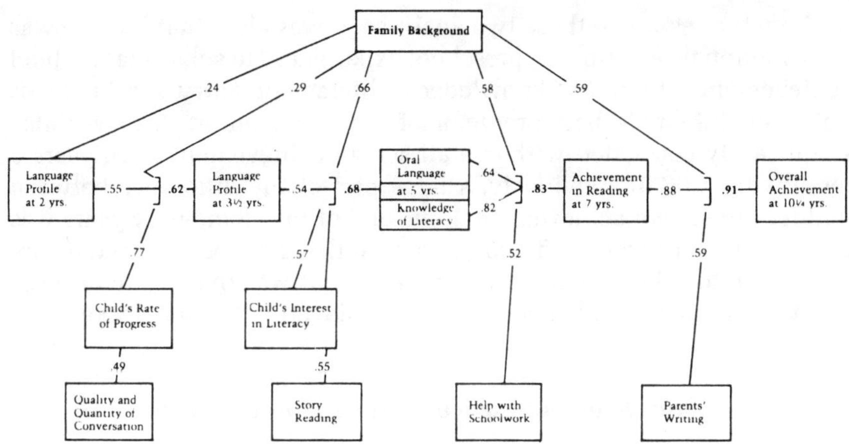

Figure 1. Predictors of School Achievement at 10 Years, 3 Months*

Multiple regression analysis was then used to find the best predictors of overall achievement at 10 years from the variables available from the previous assessment at 7 years. As can be seen from Figure 1, two variables—Achievement in Reading and Parents' Writing—yielded a multiple correlation coefficient of 0.91. Of these, achievement in reading at 7 was the single best predictor, with a correlation of 0.88. In this context, it is worth noting that, although Family Background[3] was found to be significantly correlated with overall achievement, it did not in itself account for a significant proportion of the variation remaining after Achievement in Reading at 7 years and Parents' Writing had been entered into the equation.

A similar analysis was carried out to find the best predictors of reading at 7. Again, two variables were identified: Knowledge of Literacy at 5 and Command of Oral Language at 5. These two variables yielded a multiple correlation of 0.83, with Knowledge of Literacy being the more important, with a simple correlation of 0.82. Parental Help with School Work and Family Background were both significantly correlated with Reading Achievement at 7, but neither accounted for a significant proportion of the residual variation after the first two variables had been entered into the equation.

---

* Reproduced from G. Wells, *The meaning makers*, p. 166.

[3] This variable was based on information about the occupation and terminal level of education of both parents. Details can be found in G. Wells, (1985). *Language development in the pre-school years*. Cambridge: Cambridge University Press.

From the results of these two analyses, it was clear that literacy was the common thread linking preschool experiences to subsequent school achievement. The test of knowledge of literacy on entry to school was not only the single best predictor of reading score at 7; it was also significantly correlated with overall school achievement at 10 years 3 months ($r = 0.79$). Obviously, a large part of the difference between children in school achievement at the end of the elementary years was already determined by differences in what they had experienced before they came to school. The question was: What was the nature of these crucial experiences that some children enjoyed but others lacked?

Preschool Experiences that Lead to Literacy

The Knowledge of Literacy test itself seemed to suggest that it was the concepts about print that the children had already developed by the time they entered school that made the difference, including their knowledge of the names or sounds associated with the printed forms of the letters of the alphabet. Certainly learning to read and write will involve an understanding of these formal characteristics of written language, and other research, notably that by Emilia Ferreiro and her colleagues (Ferreiro & Teberovsky, 1982), has demonstrated, first, that all children growing up in literate societies have spontaneously begun to construct hypotheses about the print forms of written language by the time they go to school and, secondly, that at that stage there are considerable differences between children in the extent of their understanding, depending on the quality and quantity of their experiences with print.

However, there is more to becoming literate than being able to handle and talk about these features of the written code, important though they are. Even more vital, we believed, was children's understanding of the *functions* of written language: the purposes that it serves in the daily lives of members of the family and the immediate community, and the value it has for them, as demonstrated by the types of "literacy events" in which these adults most frequently engage. Observation of these events provides the basis on which children construct their model of literacy, a model which is still further enriched when the children themselves become involved in some or all of these events.

In order to find out more about the range and frequency of the literacy events in which the children were themselves involved, we made use of two sources of data. First, we examined the parents' answers to the relevant questions in the interview administered when the children started school, and secondly we examined the transcripts of the recordings of spontaneous conversation made at regular intervals during the preschool years. Both sources yielded very similar evidence, but we judged that the evidence derived from the transcripts was the more reliable, as that was based on recorded events rather than on parental reports.

In almost all the homes, children were involved in a variety of literacy events, ranging from consulting the TV guide to writing letters to relatives. However, there were also obvious differences between them in the range and frequency of these activities.[4] In order to obtain an estimate of the effect of these differences on subsequent progress in the acquisition of literacy, four types of activity were selected for particular attention: looking at a picture book, drawing and coloring, listening to a story, and writing or pretending to write. The reasons for selecting these particular activities were, first, the opportunities they provided for children to discover different aspects of the use of written language and, secondly, their similarity to literacy-related activities likely to be encountered in school.

Looking at a picture book with an adult (or in some homes, a magazine or mail-order catalog) introduces him or her to the pictorial and graphic representation of meaning. In most cases, the interaction that accompanies looking at a picture book focuses on the naming game—the asking and answering of questions about the identity and attributes of the object or event depicted. This clearly prepares the child for similar question-and-answer episodes which frequently accompany or follow the reading of a story at school. Drawing and coloring were singled out for attention for two reasons: First, drawing is related to writing in being a symbolic mode of representation (cf. Vygotsky, 1978); second, in British primary schools, drawing is an integral part of the literacy learning program. The child is first asked to draw a picture and then, with the teacher's help, a caption is written underneath, which serves as a short text for reading. Both of these picture-related activities were observed to occur on several occasions in the majority of homes. Listening to a story was selected because it introduces the child to the sustained creation of meaning in the written mode. Included in this category were discussions of a story that had been read as well as actual reading episodes. The frequency with which children listened to stories read aloud varied quite considerably from home to home. Finally, writing or pretending to write. The selection of this category of literacy event requires no explanation. However, probably because of the very limited amount of

[4] Alonzo B. Anderson and Shelley J. Stokes (1984) report somewhat similar results from a study carried out in relation to pre-school children in three ethnic communities in metropolitan San Diego. Social and institutional influences on the development and practice of literacy. In H. Goelman, A. Oberg, & F. Smith (Eds.), *Awakening to literacy*. Portsmouth, NH: Heinemann Educational Books.

time that was actually recorded, only two children had engaged in this activity during the actual observations.

For each of these activities except writing, a score for each child was then calculated based on the number of occasions during the recordings on which the activity was observed. These scores were then correlated with the scores obtained on the Knowledge of Literacy test administered on entry to school, the Neale Analysis of Reading test (Neale, 1969) administered after 2 years in school, and the teachers' assessments of the children's oral language ability on entry to school. The results were very clear-cut. Only one of the preschool literacy-related activities described above was significantly related to scores on the subsequent measures, and it was related to all three of them. This was frequency of listening to a story. What these results indicate is that of the various activities investigated, it was the differences in the frequency with which children had stories read to them that best explained the differences in their subsequent achievement.

Several reasons can be suggested for this relationship and, at this stage, it is impossible to say which is the most important. Indeed, perhaps it is because so much can be learned from the story-reading experience that it is such an important introduction to literacy. First, there is the familiarity it gives with the form of written language—the structures and cadences that are to be found in the sustained meaning-making that is characteristic of writing, as distinct from those that are more typical of conversational speech. The advantage of this familiarity is that when the child encounters real books in the classroom, he or she will already be comfortable with the patterns of language that are found in them.[5] The difficulties that are encountered by children who have not had this experience are well documented by Jessie Reid's pioneering study of what young children understand about reading (1966).

The second advantage of listening to stories is the much greater breadth of experiences that the child encounters—the opportunity to go beyond the here and now of the immediate environment into other times and places, into the world of maybe and might-have-been. And of course, with these experiences comes the vocabulary for talking about them. This, I am sure, has a great deal to do with the teachers' assessments of the children's oral language ability on entry to school. Children who have had many stories read to them draw upon a much wider

---

[5] This does not apply, of course, to many of the basal readers, for the impoverished variety of language in which they are written is met in no other context. This is one of the arguments against using basal readers as the core of the reading program. An equally strong reason is that the stories they contain do not stir the reader's imagination. They offer a very feeble invitation to enter and explore an alternative possible world (cf., Bruno Bettelheim [1977]. *The uses of enchantment*. London: Thames & Hudson).

range of vocabulary when talking with their peers and teachers about many of the topics that come up in the course of classroom discussion. The effect is equally apparent in the children's dramatic play. Those who have had stories read to them explore a much wider range of situations in group play and, if one eavesdrops, one discovers many echoes of the stories they have heard. Indeed, on one occasion, I remember listening to two boys playing out a complete version of "Beauty and the Beast."

Most important, in my opinion, however, is the gradual discovery that children make of the symbolic potential of language—the power it has to represent possible objects, events, and situations that the child has never encountered. What I mean by this becomes clear if one contrasts the ways in which meanings are constructed in conversation as compared with extended written communication. To a great extent, the meanings that are exchanged in conversation—particularly the sort of conversations in which a small child is involved—arise out of and are supported by ongoing activity. Indeed, this is the basis on which children learn language in the first place. If they could not use their understanding of their conversational partner's intentions in situations of joint attention and action, they would not have any way of ever "cracking the code." In conversation, too, the meanings that are encoded in the words-in-structure are supported by other channels, such as gesture and intonation. But perhaps most important is what the participants can take for granted, as a result of previous shared experiences as well as of presently shared context. As David Olson puts it (1977), in conversation the meaning is not to be found in the spoken words alone, but in an interaction between what the speaker says, the nonverbal accompaniments, what the listener brings to the situation by way of shared knowledge and values, and the expectations set up by the situational context itself.

By contrast, the situations in which one writes are very different. Most important, writer and reader are not in face-to-face contact—indeed, the writer in many cases has no idea who the readers will be—so far fewer assumptions can be made about shared knowledge and experience. As well, there is no context of shared activity nor the support of the paralinguistic channels to provide additional cues to the reader. For all these reasons, therefore, the writer has to be much more explicit in expressing his or her meaning intentions, for the only cues that the writer can offer to the readers to help them interpret his or her meaning are those that are conveyed through the actual text. In order to understand a story, therefore, one has to learn to ignore the physical context and to pay attention to the words and structures of the text alone.

Put rather differently, one can say that, in conversation, the words spoken typically refer to an actual situation in the world that currently exists, has existed or may exist in the future, and this situation provides the context for the interpretation of what is said. However, in writing—and particularly in stories—words are most frequently used to *create* a world in the imagination, which then provides the context for interpretation. It is in this sense that writing exploits the symbolic potential of language for, through words alone, the writer can bring into existence imaginary and hypothetical worlds for the reader to enter and explore.

Becoming literate, I therefore want to suggest, concerns first and foremost learning to use language in this way, acquiring an additional "cognitive amplifier," as Jerome Bruner calls it (1966), and one that is more powerful than that made available by conversational language, for it enables the individual to become reflectively aware of his or her experiences—his knowledge—and through the manipulation of the symbols of language to then operate upon that knowledge. In my view, then, literacy and the skills of symbol manipulation that are acquired in the process of becoming fully literate are rightly treated by teachers as central in elementary education. As Margaret Donaldson puts it:

> What is going to be required for success in our educational system is that [the child] should learn to turn language and thought in upon themselves. He must become able to direct his own thought processes in a thoughtful manner. He must become able not just to talk, but to choose what he will say, not just to interpret but to weigh possible interpretations. His conceptual system must expand in the direction of increasing ability to represent itself. He must become capable of manipulating symbols. (1978, pp. 88–89)

With Donaldson, I believe that the development of this ability to operate on knowledge by means of symbols—to create possible worlds in the imagination and to modify them and test out the consequences of hypothetical actions within them—is probably the single most important achievement in education. Listening to stories read aloud is the first step along this road.

Differences in Preschool Experiences

Not all children have stories read to them, however. In our sample, fewer than half the children were read to with any frequency.[6] On the

[6] The range was from no stories at all to an average of four storyreading sessions in the 27 minutes of recorded time in each observation. On the basis of these data, it is clear that the differences between children with respect to this (as I believe, crucial) experience are very substantial indeed. While Rosie was not read to once before she went to school, Jonathan had enjoyed at least 6,000 story-reading occasions.

other hand, there may be other "literacy events" in homes and communities in which children participate and from which they can derive ideas about the purposes that written language serves and the significance it has for its users. If so, there may be other experiential bases from which to launch into literacy.

A number of recent studies suggest that this is indeed the case (Goelman et al., 1984). From the results of these studies it is now clear that, contrary to popular opinion, engagement in literacy events is not confined to the educated middle class. However, while members of literate societies make some use of their skills with written language, different cultural groups within them value literacy for different purposes and engage in somewhat different literacy practices. As a result, children growing up in such societies may develop different "models" of literacy, depending on the cultural group to which they belong. This is particularly clearly brought out in Shirley Brice Heath's ethnographic study of three communities in one urban center in the Piedmont region of the Carolinas (Heath, 1983). Two of the groups she studied were relatively self-contained working-class communities on the outskirts of the town, one black and one white. The third group consisted of members of the "mainstream" community, who were, by comparison, educated and middle-class.

Describing the experiences of children in the black working-class community, she writes:

> Just as Trackton parents do not buy special toys for their young children, they do not buy books for them either: adults do not create reading and writing tasks for the young, nor do they consciously model or demonstrate reading and writing behaviors for them. In the home, on the plaza, and in the neighborhood, children are left to find their own reading and writing tasks: distinguishing one television channel from another, knowing the name brands of cars, motorcycles and bicycles, choosing one or another can of soup or cereal, reading price tags at Mr. Dogan's store to be sure they do not pay more than they would at the supermarket. (p. 190)

Although this account starts by identifying the experiences these children do not have, we should not underrate the significance of those that they *do* have. For them, literacy is highly functional with respect to the matters that concern them: television, vehicles, shopping, and so on. And in each case, reading enables them to discriminate between categories—to make important choices. As Heath summarizes it, "children in Trackton *read to learn* before they go to school to *learn to read*" (p. 191, original emphases). Furthermore, although adults may not initiate literacy events with their children, they do respond meaningfully to the questions the children frequently ask about what some piece of print "says" by "making their instructions fit the requirements of the tasks."

In Roadville, the white working-class community, adults engage in a somewhat wider range of literacy events. The women, in particular, write notes to distant relatives and buy and sometimes read sewing patterns and home-decorating magazines. Reading and writing also occur in relation to church activities, as they do in Trackton. Unlike Trackton parents, however, the parents of Roadville children emphasize the importance of reading, and to a lesser extent of writing, and, at least in the preschool years, they act on those beliefs.

> Roadville wives and mothers buy books for their children and bring home from church special Sunday School materials supplied for the young. Before their babies are six months old, Roadville mothers read simple books, usually featuring a single object on each page, to their children. Later they choose books which tell simplified Bible stories, introduce the alphabet, numbers, or nursery rhymes; or contain "real-life" stories about boys and girls, usually taking care of their pets either at home or on a farm. When their children begin to watch *Sesame Street* and *Electric Company* on television, they buy books, games, and toys derived from these shows. They read the advertisements for other games and toys that appear on boxes the play things come in and, as their children get older, they advise them to do the same. (pp. 222–223)

For Roadville families, then, literacy has functional significance for everyday life and this is transmitted to the children. Roadville parents also seem to recognize that they have a role to play in preparing their children for the literacy demands of school, as they understand them. At the same time, there is a "closed" quality to Roadville families' encounters with print: Reading and writing are not seen as means for intellectual development.

> In Roadville, the absoluteness of ways of talking about what is written fits church ways of talking about what is written. Behind the written word is an authority, and the text is a message which can be taken apart only insofar as its analysis does not extend too far beyond the text and commonly agreed upon experiences. New syntheses and multiple interpretations create alternatives which challenge fixed roles, rules, and "rightness." (pp. 234–235)

By contrast, the third of Heath's communities—the mainstream of the nearby urban center—are much more like the parents of those children in the Bristol study who were successful in school. In these homes, attention is given to planning and following a schedule, and children are encouraged to act as conversational partners, question answerers, and information givers. There is also a general orientation to reading and writing. At an early age, children are expected to take an interest in books and information derived from books and they also see their parents reading and writing in relation to their work and leisure activities in ways that emphasize the importance of written sources of information.

As with the Bristol children, story reading is an important part of the children's experience, both at home and at Sunday school or play school, although the situations that Heath describes are more formal than those that we observed in the recordings made in our children's homes.

> Teachers and mothers expect the children to sit quietly and listen until the reader indicates that children may participate in discussion about the story. . . . The teacher usually acts as narrator for the text, and she models and questions. She asks questions about the story which directly relate to the story's content most of the time. . . . Often teachers follow up with "How do you know?" questions, in which they ask the children to identify points in the story or, more often, portions of the pictures, which let them know the location, weather, pending action, or other unexplained events of the story. (p. 254)

From these descriptions, two things are clear. On the one hand, in all three communities children participate in literacy events that are significant for community members. By the time they come to school, therefore, they all have formed ideas about the purposes that literacy serves; they have also begun to develop concepts about the medium of print itself. On the other hand, the models of literacy that children develop in the three communities are not all equally attuned to those that are typically espoused by the schools they will enter. At the end of her description of the Trackton and Roadville children's experiences, Heath concludes: "Neither community's ways with the written word prepares [the child] for the school's ways" (p. 235).

Models of Literacy at School

Since an enormous emphasis is placed in the elementary school years on helping children to become literate, one might suppose that there would be fairly universal agreement among teachers as to what being literate entails. However, from numerous discussions on this subject in which I have taken part, I am forced to conclude that this is not the case. Everyone agrees that literacy involves mastery of the written language, but that is about as far as the agreement goes.

In a recent paper (Wells, 1987), I tried to clarify the differences that had emerged in discussions by identifying four levels at which teachers may focus attention. Let me emphasize, however, that these levels do not refer to the actual processes involved in reading and writing (nor to stages in a developmental progression of learning), but rather to what is emphasized, implicitly or explicitly, in classroom instruction. The levels refer, therefore, to teacher perspectives on literacy rather than to literate behavior as such.

At the first level, which I call *performative*, the emphasis is on the graphic substance and on the mechanics of reading and writing. According to this perspective, what is involved in becoming literate is simply a matter of acquiring the skills necessary for decoding a written message to speech in order to discover its meaning, and those for encoding a spoken message in writing according to the conventions of letter formation, spelling, and punctuation. At this level, little or no attention is given to the ways in which written language differs from spoken, either in form or function, nor is there much concern with the content of what is written; instead, the emphasis is on the skills involved in efficiently handling the code.

At the second, *functional* level, the concern is with being able to cope with the literate demands that are encountered in everyday life: being able to read instructions, write a job application, or avoid being taken in by unscrupulous advertising. Those who adopt this perspective are often responding to disturbing reports concerning the scale of national or international "illiteracy"; their responsibility is often for minority groups who, for various environmental reasons, are judged likely to have difficulty in mastering the written language. In practice, teachers who emphasize the functional level of literacy tend to assume that the processes of coding and decoding have been learned; however, because they recognize that the form of written language varies according to the purpose that the writing serves, they devote much of their attention to getting students to practice on those types of texts that they judge to be functionally most important for them in life outside the school.

At the third level, the *informational*, the emphasis is on reading and writing for information. According to this perspective, literacy makes available the accumulated knowledge of the culture, particularly that enshrined in textbooks and works of reference. It is a perspective commonly found among subject-area specialists, who see their main responsibility to be the transmission of this knowledge. Reading is emphasized, with particular emphasis on a "correct" understanding of the text: writing tends to be treated as less important, and is seen largely as a means for recording what one has learned and for demonstrating that learning to others. While it is recognized that there are conventions governing appropriate forms of written language for different purposes and types of content, and that these must be learned, little attention is given to the creative intellectual processes involved, either in interpretation or in composition.

The fourth level is the *epistemic*, so-called because only at this level is due recognition given to the close relationship between the medium of language use (writing) and the way in which knowledge is constructed, modified and extended through the use of that medium. As explained earlier, by virtue of the more relaxed time frame within which reading and writing are carried out, and because of the lack of other cueing systems, the written medium demands close attention to the actual text and encourages reflection on the meanings encoded in it. Reading, and even more so writing, encourages the personal construction, evaluation, and reconstruction of knowledge. According to this perspective, therefore, to be literate is to have available and to exploit ways of generating and transforming knowledge and experience that are, in general, unavailable to those who have never learned to read and write (Olson, 1986; Scardamalia & Bereiter, 1985).

As will have become apparent, there is a relationship of inclusiveness between the four proposed levels. In the most complete literacy event, whether it involves writing or reading, the construction and critical evaluation of the text requires control of the written code, awareness of the relationship between the context of situation and the particular selection of linguistic forms, accurate and explicit matching of the actual text to the meanings to be communicated, as well as a creative and conscious exploration of the alternative possible meanings encoded in the text. Or, to put it more succinctly, to be fully literate is to be able to manage all four levels simultaneously, while giving most of one's conscious and critical attention to the symbolic world of meaning created in the text.

This may all seem somewhat abstract in the context of a consideration of children's entry into literacy, but I have two reasons for making these distinctions explicit. The first concerns the prevalent misconception that the four levels that I have outlined correspond to some sort of development progression, starting with a concern with the performative level in Grade 1 and introducing the epistemic only in the later years of high school or at university. From the evidence now available, we can say with confidence that it is not the case that children have to learn first to cope with the written code and, only when the code is mastered, can they be expected to make use of written language for the purposes of enjoyment, practical communication, or the accessing and reproduction of information. As was argued earlier, even before children can read and write for themselves, they begin to appreciate and participate in the literacy events in their communities, and where these exploit the rich symbolic potential of language—as in the collaborative exploration of a story read aloud—they are already engaging with written language at the highest, epistemic, level, albeit with as yet only limited control of the actual code. Given the opportunity, therefore, from a very early age children are able to benefit from involvement in literacy events that engage them at all four levels in the proposed model of literacy.

The second reason for identifying different emphases in the definitions that are given to "literacy" is that, to some extent, the same emphases can be found in the dominant uses that are made of literacy in different communities. From this point of view, for example, compare the three communities referred to above that were studied by Shirley Brice Heath. As a result, children come to school with rather different conceptions of the purposes that written language can serve, according to the sort of literacy events that they have most typically experienced at home in the preschool years. All such experiences are valuable, but they provide rather different starting points for teachers trying to plan programs that will enable all children to become fully literate.

Literacy Instruction in School

In the final section of this chapter, I wish to consider some of the implications of the material so far presented for the ways in which we plan opportunities for children to become literate in school. However, before doing so, I think it might be helpful to restate some of the main points of the preceding discussion.

1. The extent of a child's command of written language is the single most important predictor of his or her educational achievement at the end of the elementary years. Teachers are right, therefore, to give high priority to the acquisition of literacy in setting their goals for this stage of education.
2. The development of literacy begins in the preschool years and, in a literate society, all children have already developed some understanding of written language and the purposes that it serves before they come to school.
3. As with the development of spoken language, the early development of understanding of the form of written language takes place spontaneously and follows a common sequence, which is not dependent on deliberate or systematic instruction.
4. With respect to understanding of the functions that written language serves, however, there is much greater variation among children;

this is dependent on the sorts of literacy event that they have observed and participated in in their local communities.

5. Literacy events that emphasize all four levels in the proposed model of literacy provide the most adequate opportunities for children to become fully literate; shared story reading appears to be particularly beneficial in this respect.

If these propositions are correct, we need to reconsider the programs of instruction through which we promote the learning of literacy in the early grades. Too often, such programs are almost exclusively performative in their emphasis, conveying the impression that learning to read and write is simply a matter of learning to manage the written code. Furthermore, the approach adopted all too often assumes that children can only learn through direct instruction, and little attention is paid to the hypotheses that children have already developed spontaneously, with the result that, for many children, the teacher's efforts are at best inappropriate and at worst positively confusing.[7]

If one thing is clear, however, it is that, from the beginning, reading and writing should involve meaningful activities in which children engage because they themselves understand the purposes. As already described, some purposes will be more immediately intelligible to some children than to others as a result of their out-of-school experiences. This means that teachers need to make available a range of reading and writing activities, so that there is at least one to which each child will find it easy to relate.

Whatever their previous experiences, however, I believe all children will benefit from an introduction to literacy through stories. And this is particularly so for those who have not had this experience at home. For such children it is particularly important to make time for the one-to-one sharing of a story that was described above, for until the child has learned how to enter into the story world in one-to-one interaction

[7] Emilia Ferreiro and Ana Teberosky (1982) state the problem as follows:

> Our data reflect a long developmental process from children's initial conception of print to their final ones. This process takes place in the preschool period. Some children are at the final levels of development as they enter school. Others reach first grade at the initial levels of hypothesizing about print. The former has very little to learn in school, since first grade instruction will not challenge their capabilities. The latter group has a great deal to learn. The problem is whether traditionally conceived instruction offers them what they need.

After reviewing their evidence, they conclude that the slower developing children are actually hindered by school instruction. *Literacy before schooling*. Portsmouth, NH: Heinemann Educational Books, p. 279.

with a sympathetic adult, listening as a member of a large group may not be a very meaningful or rewarding experience.

Since finding time to read with individual children is so difficult, it is worth considering how parents can be encouraged to collaborate in this activity. One very successful approach, based on research originally carried out in Haringey, England (Hewison & Tizard, 1980), involves children in taking two books home each day, one for them to read to their parents and the other for their parents to read to them. Along with this goes the opportunity for children to buy books for themselves from the school bookshop, which is run by a group of parent volunteers.[8] In some classrooms, too, teachers have invited parents who have spare time to spend half an hour or so at the beginning or end of the session with one child or a small group of children just reading a book that one of them has chosen. It is perhaps worth noting that in one classroom, in which both these ways of inviting parental collaboration are involved, a substantial proportion of the children are not native speakers of English. For them, one-to-one interaction with an adult, centering on a shared story, provides not only an introduction to literacy but also an excellent opportunity to learn the new language as well.

Early literacy programs often concentrate on reading to the near exclusion of writing (at least of anything but the practice of letter formation). This, in my view, is a serious mistake. Recent research has shown that children are keen to start writing as soon as they come to school and that they are well able to compose stories and other forms of text even though they may as yet have only a very immature understanding of the conventions of writing (see, e.g., Bissex, 1980; Clay, 1975; Graves, 1982; Harste, Burke & Woodward, 1984). What is important about encouraging children to write at this early stage is that they are actively involved in creating their own meanings in the new medium: They discover that they too can be authors. This experience is enhanced when they see their stories "published" and other children reading them, or the instructions or notices they have written being appealed to in the regulation of classroom activities. In this way, written language becomes a purposeful means of communication for them and a source of pride as well as of enjoyment.

At the same time, as Marie Clay points out (1983), writing supports reading:

---

[8] Lists of "real" books that children at different ages are known to have found interesting and enjoyable, and suggestions to parents and teachers on how to organize a "Borrow a Book" program have been prepared by Linda Hart-Hewins and Jan Wells. Information on the scheme can be obtained from the first named author, c/o Toronto Board of Education, 155 College Street, Toronto M5T 1R1, Canada.

> If a child knows how to scan letters and words, how to study a word in order to write it and how to organize the writing of that word, he or she has the skills to deal with the detail of print. (p. 276)

In order to continue their stories, too, children will often read what they have written in order to decide how to continue, and this provides another link between production and reception—between writing and reading—in relation to topics of their own choosing.

Equally important, introducing children from the very beginning to a complete model of literacy (i.e., one that involves all four levels from performative to epistemic) ensures that reading and writing are integrated with uses of spoken language and that all four language processes are seen, not as ends in themselves, but as means for thinking, feeling, and communicating in the achievement of purposes that children have made their own. With the youngest children, this can be achieved through group planning and implementation of such activities as setting up a cafe or hospital or carrying out a research project on shells or wild and domestic animals (McKenzie, 1985). Books are written, read, and consulted by children in the course of engaging in these activities and, equally naturally, they talk with each other and with their teacher about the purpose and significance of what they have read and written.

With somewhat older children, the same effects can be achieved by organizing the curriculum around themes which allow for a variety of individual or small group projects. Such thematic work can start with a class brainstorming session in which possible topics for investigation are considered and selected. Within the resulting negotiated framework, individuals or small groups of children are then responsible for researching their chosen topics and deciding how to present the results of their research. Periodic sharing times ensure that the individual expertise that is being gained is made available to others and that links and connections between the various projects are explored. Finally, the various strands can be brought together in the form of an exhibition, or even better, an "open house," at which the children are present and talk about their work to other classes or to their parents and other visitors to the school (Wells, 1986, chap. 10).

Having seen several examples of thematic work carried out in this way, I am convinced that this is one of the most effective ways of enabling children to become fully literate. It also has the advantage of helping them to become active constructors of their own knowledge in relation to other areas of the curriculum. However, it does call for a different understanding of the teacher's role from that which is held by those who see themselves as trainers of skills and transmitters of knowledge. Where learning is recognized to be a collaborative activity, in which the child is an active and creative partner, the teacher's role is preeminently that of motivator and guide, helping children to select, plan, and execute their own learning tasks and, in the process, to develop conscious and deliberate control over the cognitive, affective, and communicative strategies that these tasks require. Clearly, the performance of this role demands considerable skill in one-to-one interaction, or "conferencing" as it is sometimes called, and most of us still have much to learn in this area.

Balancing this responsibility to respond contingently to the interests and needs of individual children is a second and equally important responsibility: ensuring that, over time, the learning of both individuals and the whole class becomes more systematic, and that they encounter and make their own the knowledge, values, and skills that are considered important within our culture.

There is no doubt that this conception of the teacher's role is a demanding one, calling for a wide range of knowledge and skills and a willingness to be flexible in forward planning in order to make the most of emergent opportunities as they arise. What makes it more difficult is that there is no blueprint for success—no guidelines or set of instructions that will provide "correct" answers for all the decisions that must be made in the course of each day. However, where teachers see their classrooms as learning environments for themselves as well as for their students, and where staff rooms are places in which the fruits of such learning are shared and collaboratively evaluated, a climate of joint enquiry and mutual support will be established in which individual teachers feel able to take the risks that are necessary for any real personal or professional growth.

References

Anderson, A. B. & Stokes, S. J. (1984). Social and institutional influences on the development and practice of literacy. In H. Goelman, A. Oberg, & F. Smith (Eds.), *Awakening to literacy*. Portsmouth, NH: Heinemann Educational Books.

Bettelheim, B. (1977). *The uses of enchantment*. London: Thames & Hudson.

Bissex, G. (1980). *Gnys at wrk: A child learns to read and write*. Cambridge, MA: Harvard University Press.

Bruner, J. S. (1966). On cognitive growth. In J. S. Bruner et al. (Eds.), *Studies in cognitive growth*. New York: Wiley.

Clay, M. (1975). *What did I write?* London: Heinemann Educational Books.

Clay, M. (1983). Getting a theory of writing. In B. Kroll & G. Wells (Eds.), *Explorations in the development of writing*. New York: Wiley.

Donaldson, M. (1978). *Children's minds*. London: Fontana.

Ferreiro, E. & Teberosky, A. (1982). *Literacy before schooling*. Portsmouth, NH: Heinemann Educational Books.

Goelman, H., Oberg, A. & Smith, F. (Eds.) (1984) *Awakening to literacy*. Portsmouth, NH: Heinemann Educational Books.

Graves, D. (1982). *Writing: Teachers and children at work*. Portsmouth, NH: Heinemann Educational Books.

Harste, J., Burke, C. & Woodward, V. (1984). *Language stories and literacy lessons*. Portsmouth, NH: Heinemann Educational Books.

Heath, S. B. (1983). *Ways with words*. New York: Cambridge University Press.

Hewison, J. & Tizard, J. (1980). Parental involvement and reading attainment. *British Journal of Educational Psychology, 50*, 209–215.

McKenzie, M. (1985). Classroom contexts for language and literacy. In A. Jaggar and M.T. Smith-Burke, (Eds.), *Observing the language learner*. IRA and NCTE.

Neale, M. (1969). *Neale analysis of reading* (2nd ed.). Basingstoke, Hants.: Macmillan Education.

Olson, D. (1977). From utterance to text: The bias of language in speech and writing. *Harvard Educational Review 47*(3), 257–281.

Olson, D. (1986). The cognitive consequences of literacy. *Canadian Psychology, 27*(2), 109–121.

Reid, J. (1966). Learning to think about reading. *Educational Research*, 9, 56–62.

Scardamalia, M. & Bereiter, C. (1985). Development of dialectical processes in composition. In D. Olson, N. Torrance, & A. Hildyard, (Eds.), *Literacy, language and learning*. New York: Cambridge University Press.

Vygotsky, L. (1978). *Mind in society*. Cambridge, MA: Harvard University Press.

Wells, G. (1985). *Language development in the pre-school years*. Cambridge: Cambridge University Press.

Wells, G. (1986). *The meaning makers*. Portsmouth, NH: Heinemann Educational Books.

Wells, G. (1987). Apprenticeship in literacy. *Interchange 18*(1/2), 109–123. Toronto: The Ontario Institute for Studies in Education.

Chapter 3

The Beginnings of Writing

Glenda L. Bissex

Norwich University

This is a story about learning to write. It was told by Rudyard Kipling in his *Just so stories* about a young neolithic girl named Taffy who is, as we meet her, carp fishing with her father, Tegumai:

> Taffy took a marrow-bone and sat mousy-quiet for ten whole minutes, while her Daddy scratched on pieces of birch-bark with a shark's tooth. Then she said, "Daddy, I've thinked of a secret surprise. You make a noise—any sort of noise."
>
> "Ah!" said Tegumai. "Will that do to begin with?"
>
> "Yes," said Taffy. "You look just like a carpfish with its mouth open. Say it again, please."
>
> "Ah! ah! ah!" said her Daddy. "Don't be rude, my daughter."
>
> "I'm not meaning rude, really and truly," said Taffy. "It's part of my secret-surprise-think. *Do* say *ah*, Daddy, and keep your mouth open at the end, and lend me that tooth. I'm going to draw a carp-fish's mouth wide-open."
>
> "What for?" said her Daddy.
>
> "Don't you see?," said Taffy, scratching away on the bark. "That will be our little secret s'prise. When I draw a carp-fish with his mouth open in the smoke at the back of our Cave—if Mummy doesn't mind—it will remind you of that ah—noise. Then we can play that it was me jumped out of the dark and s'prised you with that noise—same as I did in the beaver-swamp last winter."
>
> "Really?" said her Daddy, in the voice that grown-ups use when they are truly attending. "Go on, Taffy."
>
> "Oh bother!" she said. "I can't draw all of a carp-fish but I can draw something that means a carp-fish's mouth. Don't you know how they stand on their heads rooting in the mud? Well, here's a pretence carp-fish (we can play that the rest of him is drawn). Here's just his mouth, and that means *ah*." And she drew this.

Figure 1.

"That's not bad," said Tegumai, and scratched on his own piece of bark for himself; "but you've forgotten the feeler that hangs across his mouth."

"But I can't draw, Daddy."

"You needn't draw anything of him except just the opening of his mouth and the feeler across. Then we'll know he's a carp-fish 'cause the perches and trouts haven't got feelers. Look here, Taffy." And he drew this.

Figure 2.

"Now I'll copy it," said Taffy. "Will you understand *this* when you see it?" And she drew this.

Figure 3.

"Perfectly," said her Daddy, "And I'll be quite as s'prised when I see it anywhere, as if you had jumped out from behind a tree and said 'Ah!' "

"Now make another noise," said Taffy, very proud.

"Yah!" said her Daddy, very loud.

"H'm," said Taffy. "That's a mixy noise. The end part is *ah*-carp-fish-mouth; but what can we do about the front part? *Yer-yer-yer* and *ah*! *Ya*!"

"It's very like the carp-fish-mouth noise. Let's draw another bit of the carp-fish and join 'em," said her Daddy. *He* was quite incited too.

"No. If they're joined, I'll forget. Draw it separate. Draw his tail. If he's standing on his head the tail will come first. 'Sides, I think I can draw tails easiest," said Taffy.

"A good notion," said Tegumai. "Here's a carp-fish tail for the *yer*-noise." And he drew this.

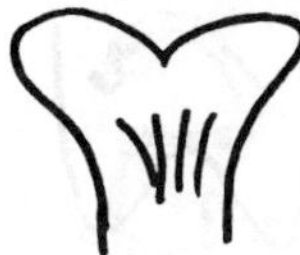

Figure 4.

"I'll try now," said Taffy. " 'Member I can't draw like you, Daddy. Will it do if I just draw the split part of the tail, and the stickydown line for where it joins?" And she drew this.

Figure 5.

Her Daddy nodded, and his eyes were shiny bright with 'citement.
"That's beautiful," she said. "Now make another noise, Daddy."
"Oh!," said her Daddy, very loud.
"That's quite easy," said Taffy. "You make your mouth all around like an egg or a stone. So an egg or a stone will do for that."
"You can't always find eggs or stones. We'll have to scratch a round something like one." And he drew this.

Figure 6.

"My gracious!" said Taffy, "what a lot of noise-pictures we've made,—carp-mouth, carp-tail, and egg! Now, make another noise, Daddy."
"Ssh!" said her Daddy, and frowned to himself, but Taffy was too incited to notice.
"That's quite easy," she said, scratching on the bark.
"Eh, what?" said her Daddy, "I meant I was thinking, and didn't want to be disturbed."
"It's a noise just the same. It's the noise a snake makes, Daddy, when it is thinking and doesn't want to be disturbed. Let's make the *ssh*-noise a snake. Will this do?" And she drew this.

Figure 7.

"There," she said. "That's another s'prise-secret. When you draw a hissy-snake by the door of your little back-cave where you mend the spears, I'll know you're thinking hard; and I'll come in most mousy-quiet. And if you draw it on a tree by the river when you're fishing, I'll know you want me to walk most *most* mousy-quiet, so as not to shake the banks."
"Perfectly true," said Tegumai. "And there's more in this game than you think. Taffy, dear, I've a notion that your Daddy's daughter has hit upon the finest thing that there ever was since the Tribe of Tegumai took to using shark's teeth instead of flints for their spear-heads. I believe we've found out *the* big secret of the world."
"Why?" said Taffy, and her eyes shone too with incitement.
"I'll show," said her Daddy. "What's water in the Tegumai language?"
"*Ya*, of course, and it means river too—like Wagai-*ya*—the Ulagai river."
"What is bad water that gives you a fever if you drink it—black water—swamp-water?"
"*Yo*, of course."
"Now look," said her Daddy. "S'pose you saw this scratched by the side of a pool in the beaver-swamp?" And he drew this.

Figure 8.

"Carp-tail and round egg. Two noises mixed! *Yo*, bad water," said Taffy. " 'Course I wouldn't drink that water because I'd know you said it was bad."
"But I needn't be near the water at all. I might be miles away, hunting, and still—"
"And *still* it would be just the same as if you stood there and said, 'G'way, Taffy, or you'll get fever.' All that in a carp-fish tail and a round egg! O Daddy, we must tell Mummy quick!" and Taffy danced all round him. . . . (pp. 120–126)

Learning to Write in School

Let's look at another scene for learning to write. It is one of many nearly identical rooms in a large building. Inside the room are many children, sitting at little tables, and one grown-up who is standing. The children are very quiet. The grown-up is talking and she is drawing something between two horizontal lines on a chalkboard. It's the letter A. She is showing the children exactly how to draw the letter themselves, and now the children pick up their pencils and make strings of A's between the lines on their paper. Sometimes they do not keep within the lines. Sometimes they do not start their letter A's at the same place the grown-up did. She walks around and sees what they are doing. She tells them that their letters are nice or she explains what's wrong with them. She does not look as though she enjoys this. Neither do the children. Now she gathers up all their papers and puts them in a pile on her desk.

In another nearly identical room hangs a big picture of Miss Munchy Mouth and also a big cardboard letter M. The children all say together with their teacher, "Munchy Mouth, Munchy Mouth, Munchy Mouth."
"What letter does Munchy Mouth begin with?" the teacher asks them.
"M," many of them say.
"And what does the letter M say?" asks the teacher.
"Mmm," say some of the children.
"That's right—mmm," says their teacher, "Let's all say it again: mmm. Good." Then she hands out a drawing of Miss Munchy Mouth for them to color. When they are finished coloring, she gathers the papers and puts them in a pile on her desk.

In another nearly identical room, the teacher has written a paragraph on the chalkboard which the children are copying onto their papers. They are so busy trying to copy the letters correctly that some of them overlook the spaces between the letters. When the teacher sees they have left out spaces, he shows them how to put two fingers on their paper at the end of every word in order to leave the right amount of space. They thought their task was to copy the letters; copying the spaces doesn't make sense to them. When they are through copying, they give their papers to the teacher, who piles them on his desk.

In another room, the teacher has been questioning the children about a trip they took the day before. She writes some of the key words from their discussion on the chalkboard. Then she tells the children to each write a story about their trip. She reminds them that some of the words they may want to use are on the board. When they want to write other words that they don't know how to spell, they raise their hands and she will come and write the word for them in their individual spelling books. The children who aren't sure how to spell many words spend most of their writing time with their hands in the air, waiting for the busy teacher to get to them. They have to keep trying to remember what it was they wanted to say using the word they can't spell. When writing time is over, the children pass their papers to the end of each row, where the teacher picks them up and puts them in a basket on her desk.

Writing Environments Compared

In these scenes for learning to write—Kipling's fantasy of neolithic home teaching and my stereotypes of a modern, teacher-centered school—we see very different child–adult relationships. Tegumai and Taffy are collaborators in a joint enterprise. They listen to and build on one another's ideas and knowledge. ("'Really?' said her Daddy in the voice that grown-ups use when they are truly attending. 'Go on, Taffy.'" She draws the carp head and he adds the feeler.) They are partners in a dialogue. The difference between their abilities to draw does not diminish the child's contribution. Her simplification of the carp's tail (because she "can't draw") creates the letter Y.

In traditional classrooms, teachers instruct. They stand up and talk while the children seated below listen. They ask questions, but questions to which they already know the answers. They listen to the children, but generally to see if their responses are correct. The teachers are supplying the IMPORTANT information. When they teach sound–letter correspondences, they start from the letters, which seem the logical point: letters have sounds. But this is the perspective of adults who already know the written language. What children know—and are more keenly aware of than adults—is the sound system of the language. Children's invented spellings can reveal their keen perceptions of speech sounds, as when they spell *day* DA but *dragon* JRAGIN. If you say those two words aloud, you hear and you feel in the position of your mouth and tongue the differences in the initial *d* sound, which young spellers often represent although our spelling system disregards them. The point is that children come to school with forms of knowledge that can be built on—knowledge that should make literacy learning more sensible and efficient for them—if we enable them to show us what they know already.

The purpose for writing in the modern classroom is quite different from that in the neolithic "classroom." A functional purpose for writing is clear from the start in Taffy's "secret surprise" notion. The drawing of the carp's mouth will re-create an incident where she jumped out of the dark and surprised her father with an *ah*-noise. He affirms that function of writing when he says, "And I'll be quite as s'prised when

I see it anywhere, as if you had jumped out from behind a tree and said 'Ah!' " Taffy immediately sees uses for the snake noise—a message for her to be quiet while her father is mending spears or is fishing. This writing, they know, will be a part of and make a difference in their lives, especially the ability to warn of danger through writing without being present in person. In contrast, the writings in the traditional classroom end up in piles on the teacher's desk. Their purpose is practice—dummy runs; their aim is to be correct, not to communicate.

Taffy is learning by inventing—she and her Daddy are inventing the alphabet and its uses—while children in a traditional classroom are receiving established knowledge. But the research of Emilia Ferreiro (1982) shows us that established knowledge about literacy is not simply handed down to children. When children learn to write, they reinvent the writing system. Ferreiro's studies of 3- to 6-year-olds reveal that when they first write, children will represent an object by a single, letter-like shape. Then, moving closer to our writing system, they will use a combination of several varied shapes to represent a name. For some time, the number of letter-like forms required for a word corresponds to the size or quantity of the object named: more letters for a big horse than for a small chicken and more for *carrots* than for a single *carrot*. Only after trying out this theory do children discover the correspondence between writing and speech, first reasoning that letters represent syllables and, finally, that they represent sounds. Children puzzle over the relationship between print and meaning or speech before schooling compels them to do so, and their understanding evolves through a series of hypotheses about that relationship. Many of the theories they try out and the conventions they invent (such as separating words by dots, writing from right to left, and using one letter for each syllable) are or were used in other written language systems. Children do not leap from illiteracy to an understanding that our writing system is alphabetic when they receive their first phonics lesson.

To learn is to reinvent, said Piaget. Why reinvent the wheel? To make it our own and to truly know it. Said Ferreiro (1984):

> Either we conceive literacy development as the acquisition of a set of marks, the functions of which become clear through social experiences while the structure remains opaque *or* we admit that the structure of the system (more precisely, the reconstruction of it as a system) is a necessary part of the ownership process. Children pose deep questions to themselves. Their problems are not solved when they succeed in meaningfully identifying a letter or a string of letters, because they try to understand not only the elements or the results but also, and above all, the very nature of the system. (p. 172)

Meanwhile, in the traditional classrooms, teachers are asking much less profound questions of the children: "What does the letter M say?" or "How do you spell *dog*?" They are checking whether the children remember what they have been taught.

Another benefit of reinventing the wheel is the excitement and power of discovery. Taffy dances around her father and wants to "tell Mummy quick!" Her Daddy, grasping further implications of his daughter's invention, believes they have "found out *the* big secret of the world." The feelings of excitement and power are fuel for new discoveries and learning.

The children in the classrooms sit as quietly as they can at their desks. Their teachers know it's important that they learn to spell and write. There are tests, checklists, the judgments of next year's teachers, the principal's evaluation, parents' expectations—all crowding between each teacher and the children. There seems no space for discovery and for the risks of making mistakes that go along with the freedom to discover. Instruction appears surer, more efficient, although teachers may have to "motivate" the children, in an effort to supply the kind of energy that Taffy herself was generating from her learning. But after all, our writing system already exists, and the teacher's job is to explain it to the children and see that they practice it correctly. This is solemn work. For the children, however, the writing system, in a sense, may not yet exist. Where is the joy the teacher might have felt in sharing in the students' discoveries? Where is the children's sense of ownership and power in their own intellectual processes, a power they must have felt in learning to speak?

What I'm suggesting about the relationship between teacher and child, about the purpose for learning, about the way learning takes place and the emotional atmosphere created, sounds very idealistic, even impossible, doesn't it? You can't take each one of your 20 or 30 students on a long fishing trip and leave the rest behind. But teaching in ways that make use of children's existing knowledge and strategies for learning, that are energized by children's excitement in making discoveries and by teachers' joy in sharing that excitement isn't idealistic: It's efficient and practical. It does not waste human resources.

We have for too long identified literacy learning with particular methods of instruction—methods that have more to do with the structure of traditional schooling than with the nature of learning. Although schools cannot be restructured overnight, all teachers have some degree of freedom to shape what goes on in their classrooms and what goes on in their heads—how they *see* teaching and learning. A change of vision can transform the whole atmosphere of a classroom. I have seen it happen. So it is not useless for teachers to reflect on how children learn language in the first place—on some of the knowledge and successful learning strategies they bring to school with them—and how these may inform the teaching of writing.

Lessons from Learning to Talk

Children learn to talk by talking, by being talked to, by asking questions and by listening to others talking. They see the functions and values of speech; they receive feedback and encouragement in their own efforts. They learn to talk by interacting with an environment that provides rich information about language. Some people believe that all children learn to speak because speech is somehow "natural" for us as humans while writing (and with it, of course, reading) is not "natural." But those very few children that we know of who have grown up in isolation from human society, and thus from human language, have not grown up speaking.

We may underestimate the spontaneity and strength of the urge to write among children growing up in a literate society. My undergraduate students at Johnson State College, who recalled this aspect of their childhoods more vividly than I, taught me a lesson about the importance of writing. Here are some of their astonishingly clear memories:

> I started writing as soon as I could hold a pencil. I can remember sitting up in my highchair with the tray up, working on my homework, like my brothers and sisters. I would yell to my mother, "Is P-T-O right?" and she would say, "Yes, I guess so." I would say, "Yes, P-T-O is right," and go on pretending to do my homework. The only word I thought I could spell right was PTO, which I later learned wasn't even a word.

> I can remember wanting to learn to write so badly! I would watch my brothers and sisters as they scribbled nonsense on paper. They looked so official, so grown up. I would imitate their grandeur. I quite often played "restaurant" where I would "write" orders on paper and hand them in to the "chef."

> My writing career began at an early age. When I was a pre-schooler, I would study my older brother's school papers. The thing that intrigued me most was the letter C, which the teacher used to indicate that the paper was correct. I worked on making my own C's. I practiced them in orange crayon all over the bathroom walls in our house.

> I remember, before school years, doing a lot of scribbling. Although this scribbling meant nothing to my family, I can recall being able to read the whole thing. As the family giggled and thought how "cute" it was, I would sit in my chair and read my scribbles.

> Since I can remember, I wrote. I remember taking crayons and writing on the walls, and my mother would yell at me because it was scribbling. But would it be funny if I wrote a word; she probably wouldn't have yelled at me then. I really remember wanting to express with my pencil, pen, or whatever, but I couldn't—no one understood!
>
> When I became aware of letters I was amazed, and I learned to write words. I remember my teachers making me always write in pencil because I'd have to erase my errors. I always wished it could have been in pen so I could just keep writing without stopping.

Children learn to write by writing in an environment that is full of writing, just as children learn to talk by talking in an environment that is full of talk. Today more and more students of all ages are learning to write by writing every day in classrooms that are full of writing in progress as well as finished products: classrooms where teachers are writing, too, sharing their drafts and writing problems with their students; classrooms where young writers are talking with one another about their writing as they become constructively critical readers and listeners; classrooms where books are seen as resources for young authors to learn about the craft from more experienced authors. Students know that a reader, not merely a corrector, will receive their writing and that those pages are not exercises. Through the power of their own experience, they come to understand that writing conveys, above all, meanings.

To try to express ourselves and yet not be understood is one of the griefs of human life, for children no less than for adults. It is painful to be unheard, and it is painful to be told we are wrong. Young children learning to talk at home are fortunate because their families respond first of all to their meanings, not to their errors. Families are eager to attach meanings to babies' first speech sounds. They do not immediately correct a beginning speaker's misarticulations; in fact they sometimes find them charming and imitate them. They do not insist that beginning speakers talk in complete sentences, but may expand children's one- or two-word sentences into full statements to check if they have understood them as intended. How differently beginning writers are treated in some classrooms!

One first grader had a "dictionary" in which his teacher recorded words he needed to have spelled for his writing. Since he had been writing at home for more than a year and was spelling many words conventionally, I was surprised to find the word *dog*, one of the first he'd learned, in his dictionary. I asked him if he didn't know it already, and he said, "Yes, but I didn't know how to make the g right." At home he had written prolifically and tried many kinds of writing; at school he wrote one sentence on the few lines beneath his drawing the way his classmates did. As he must have seen it, writing at school meant correctly forming letters to make correctly spelled words on the lines. He spent most of his writing time, instead, elaborating his drawings, for which there were not expectations of correctness.

In contrast, beginning writers in a different kind of classroom write notes to their teacher, to each other and to pen pals, all of whom respond to their messages. They write journals in which their teacher writes comments about what they've said. They write books that their classmates read. They know they are writing messages—meanings—and their skills advance through constant practice in an environment rich with information about print and language, and through the genuine motivation of being understood.

Children learn language—written or spoken—among people who respond to meaning before form. This is also a premise of writing conferences, which focus on developing and clarifying the content of a piece before editing the language. In a primary classroom, Tiffany reads aloud to Amy her story about some mice who are chasing another mouse. After she's heard the whole story, Amy asks Tiffany, "Why don't you tell what happened to the other mice?"

"That's a good idea," Tiffany agrees.

"'Cause how would I know that?" continues Amy. "They ran after him, but what did they do after that?"

"I guess they just ran back 'cause they knew he was too far away to catch him," answered Tiffany who, after thinking about it a little more, added to her story: "The other mice were running back to have a drink." If Tiffany decides to publish this story for her classmates, her teacher will have an editing conference with her, where she is helped to make corrections for her larger audience.

Good writers, viewing writing as expression and communication, focus first on meaning, while poor writers, viewing the aim of writing as correctness, focus from the start on avoiding errors. Their premature corrections break the flow of their writing and thinking, and usually do not achieve their error-free aim. Of course correctness is desirable, but stressing it before meaning confuses the means with the ends of writing, like sounding the right notes but missing the music.

Teachers often are concerned about correctness because they fear children will learn bad habits if errors are not pointed out and corrected at once. In adults, errors often *have* become habits; but if you closely observe young children's writings, you will see how flexible and experimental their learning is—how aware they are of their errors, and how they move ever closer to conventionality through their own efforts. For example, here is how the spelling of the word *directions* evolved over 3 years in the writings of one child:

DRAKTHENS (5 years, 7 months)
DRAKSHINS (5 years, 8 months)
DIRECKSHONS (7 years, 5 months)
DIREKSHONS (7 years, 5 months)
DIRECTIONS or DIRECTOINS (8 years, 1 month)
DIRECTIONS (8 years, 7 months)

Children can be taught to be poor writers or good writers. The role of the teacher is crucial, especially for children who have less opportunity or inclination to learn to write at home.

Before children speak words, they intone sentences; they practice the overall shapes of sentences before they differentiate words. A similar thing happens in the process of learning to read: Before children recognize or decode words, they pretend-read books, turning the pages while retelling a familiar story. Or they get the main point from print they see around them, as children who say that the brand name on a tube of toothpaste says "toothpaste" before they are aware of sound-letter correspondences. Before printing individual letter forms, children often write strings of letter-like shapes. How much these so-called scribblings express the children's knowledge about writing is evident in examples of 4-year-olds' writing from the research of Harste, Burke, and Woodward (1984, p. 92):

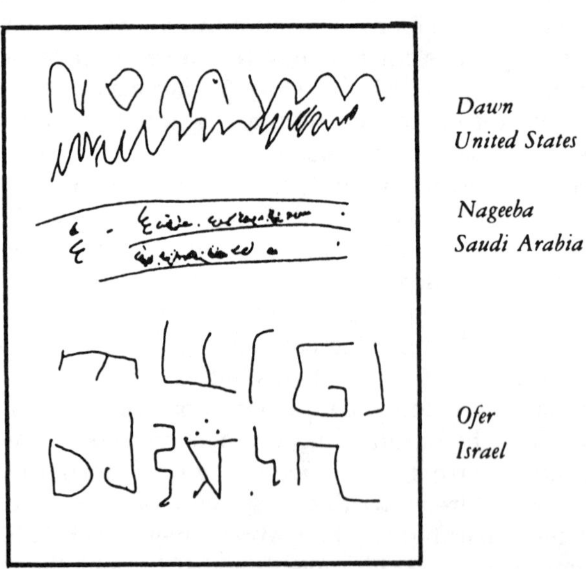

Figure 9.

Clearly these young writers have a global sense of the configuration of their culture's writing system. This global sense is the foundation for their later differentiation of smaller units, of letters and words.

Just as children's language learning moves from global to differentiated forms, it moves from fundamentals toward refinements. In learning to speak, children grasp very early the fundamental distinction between consonants and vowels—between closed sounds and open sounds. This distinction is maximized between the most closed consonant sound (m) and the most open vowel sound (a), so it is not surprising that *mama* is quite a universal baby word. In learning to write, children very early—as young as 3 years—distinguish between writing and drawing, even while they are still scribbling, as the research of Harste et al. has revealed. Drawings are generally global, centered on the paper, and connected, while writings are linear, spaced, and located off center when they are done on the same page as drawings.

When children begin to speak, in one- and two-word sentences, they choose the most important words: "Truck" may mean "I hear a truck going by"; "Owen eat" may mean "Owen wants to eat now." Similarly, when children begin to write phonetically, they represent the most important sounds in the most significant words. In invented spellings, more and more of the omitted speech sounds become represented as children's skills develop. Their texts often grow in the same way, with ever more of the less essential omitted words materializing over time. This sort of development can be seen in some writings by first graders in September:

> Jamie drew a monster (labeled MSTR) standing beside his cave (CAV). He chose the most important and concrete words to write; the rest of the text emerged when he told his teacher his paper said "This monster lives in a cave."
>
> On the first day of school Jennifer drew a house and wrote H. The next week both her drawings and writing were elaborated: a house (HS) with a smoking chimney and a lawn in front on which stood two smiling figures, Mary (M) and ME. She told her teacher it said, "I am at my friend Mary's house."
>
> An 8-year-old with a learning problem who is also in this classroom shows the same pattern of development. The first day of school he drew a square green wagon with a large wheel (labeled WE) and dictated, "My wagon has wheels." The next week he drew a pelican (PLEN) in wavy water (WTR) with a dock (DC) at one edge of it: "I saw a pelican in Florida near the dock." Toward the end of September his sentence was fully represented in writing: THE FIS IS IN THE WATR.

Figure 10.

Language—both spoken and written—develops from a sense of the whole toward an understanding of how its parts function, and from a grasp of the most fundamental distinctions toward ever finer ones. It is learned among people who attend to meaning before form. And it is learned in a language environment, not merely by imitation but by re-creation—by constructing and testing rules. That is, children learn language not just as little mimics but as little scientists. Each child needs to make sense for herself or himself of how language works.

Children seem to have a built-in learning process that is more unfailing than the adult logic of scope and sequence charts and mastery learning. We may come to see and to trust children's learning more by taking time to observe rather than always instructing—by taking time to be instructed ourselves by children so that, eventually, we may teach them better.

Observing Beginning Writers

I spent 3 years observing in classrooms, as researcher with the Vermont Writing Program. (And "observing" for me included working with children and talking with teachers to learn how they received what was happening.) It was exciting work—except for my experiences in one particular classroom, where I began to feel disappointed with myself and frustrated that I wasn't learning more about the children's writing development. Eventually I figured out that the more the teacher assigned topics for writing, structured the assignments into short answer responses, and depended on workbook exercises, the less room existed for the children to show their development. Their writings looked more and more alike, were less and less interesting and informative for me, and generated less excitement from them. They were filling in the blanks, not creating. Thus a prime condition for observing children's growth through writing is an environment that allows space and visibility for that growth.

Some teachers give their students blank journals, or sheets of plain paper, or a choice between stapled booklets or single sheets of paper all of different sizes. They ask the children—even if they are first graders on the first day of school—to write. This is the children's first step in showing what they know, and their responses usually vary widely: 6-year-olds, for instance, may simply draw, or write their names, or make strings of letters and numbers, or add some words to their drawings, or write a story in invented spellings. The teachers circulate around the room to observe how the children are writing. Are they sounding out spellings? (Often you can overhear them sounding aloud.) Which children are not yet using letters to represent sounds but rather are showing their visual knowledge of print by writing strings of letters or other symbols? Are children writing from left to right and from the top to the bottom of the page? What information about spellings or letter formation are they asking for and giving one another? Which children are able to read back what they have written? (Beginning inventive spellers often have difficulty here.) Do some writers make self-corrections and revisions as they work? How long can they stay engaged with writing? Have children memorized the spellings of some words beyond their names? Teachers ask children how they learned those words and find out about their other resources for literacy learning: reading materials, parents, siblings, and the like. They watch, listen, question, and ask children to tell about their writings.

When children choose their own topics for writing or drawing, teachers learn much about their students' concerns and interests, about their lives as well as their skills. Teachers can then find the common ground between their own knowledge and their students' knowledge, between their own lives and their students' lives, where they can meet those children and thus truly teach.

When children are asked to show what they know, their responses are more diverse than can be revealed through tests or exercises. Having evidence of how different children are at the beginning of school, teachers will not expect them to be at the same, standardized place in their writing development by the end of the year. They will expect children to grow and learn, and will see their essential role as being responsible for children's *learning* rather than for *teaching* in the sense of correcting errors and covering a predetermined curriculum.

When we appreciate the depth of children's understanding—how they start from the most fundamental and difficult questions about literacy, when we understand how much they need to know and do, in fact, learn beyond what is in our lesson plans and textbooks and worksheets, then we become more aware of the many ways in which we teach. We teach by allowing children the freedom to ask their own questions and to guide their own learning, where they can, and to inform us when they need help. We teach by providing a literate environment that evokes children's questions about print and draws them toward using print. We teach by confirming what children already know—the knowledge they can build on—as well as by supplying new information and thoughtful questions.

When we observe and listen to children, when we are in touch with what they know and how they are learning, we can teach *with* them rather than *at* them.

Doing–to and Doing–with

The doing-to model denies or neglects the energy of the children as collaborators in the learning process. Teachers then must supply the energy for learning—that is, must "motivate" the students. Everything comes from above: the knowledge, the drive, the decisions about what shall be learned and when. Providing all this energy may cause teachers to burn out. The doing-to model is a model of disempowerment, creating dependent learners and disempowering teachers as well, as they become monitors and managers of other people's programs or "learning systems."

There is no prescription for the doing-with model of teaching. It uses many different types of teachers: printed materials and print in the environment, the knowledge and questions of other children in the classroom, of adults, and of the learner himself or herself. It requires faith in children's desire and ability to learn, and faith in what they know already—faith in their natural learning systems. It requires teachers' faith in their own ability to educate, for the ultimate responsibility is not with some expert's program, workbook series, or curriculum guide. It is with YOU. And with the children who will come to share with you the responsibility for their learning.

The rewards of doing-with teaching are the excitement and joy of collaborating in momentous discoveries. Like Taffy's Daddy, Tegumai, you will never be bored or burned out!

References

Ferreiro, E. (1982). The relationship between oral and written language: The children's viewpoints. In Y. Goodman, M. Haussler, & D. Strickland (Eds.), *Oral and written language development research: Impact on the schools*. Urbana, IL: National Council of Teachers of English.

Ferreiro, E. (1984). The underlying logic of development. In H. Goelman, A. Oberg, & F. Smith (Eds.), *Awakening to literacy*. Exeter, NH: Heinemann.

Harste, J., Burke, C., & Woodward, V. (1984). *Language stories and literacy lessons*. Portsmouth, NH: Heinemann.

Kipling, R. (1978). How the alphabet was made. In *Just so stories*. New York: Weathervane Books. (Originally published, 1902.)

Chapter 4

Early Reading

Carolyn N. Hedley

Fordham University

Judith Newman (1985) states in the book *Whole language: Theory in use:* "Not until we were able to appreciate the complexity of children's oral language development did it become possible for us to consider young children's awareness of and interaction with written language." In her review of the literature on the topic, she cites many experts who have come to the conclusion that children's language knowledge includes knowledge of the written code. Children find that written language makes sense, that it contains messages, and they "write" and "read" profusely when provided with message making materials and given the freedom to explore them. Sometimes pictures or photographs are a first message, but very young children, of 2, 3, and 4 years of age also enjoy working with written forms of symbolic experience (Clay, 1985; Durkin, 1982; Harste, Woodward, & Burke, 1984; Potter, 1986). Research is proving that children are able to use visual strategies to discover how "print" operates (Ferreiro & Teberosky, 1982; Holdaway, 1983). The validity of early reading programs and children's ability to deal with print in relaxed, informal ways using integrative "whole language" approaches has been established in the research on language and literacy development.

Early Childhood Programs and Reading

The efficacy of early childhood programs is incontrovertible; longitudinal studies have repeatedly demonstrated the benefits of early education to children's social, linguistic, and personal development. Furthermore, those programs with strong language development components as well as other developmental tasks have benefited children throughout their school years and into their adult lives (Consortium for Longitudinal Studies, 1983). An article in the *New York Times* (July 24, 1986) reports that the President of the Board of Education of the New York City public schools, Robert Wagner, has vowed that all 4-year-olds will be in the schools by 1989.

Early childhood programs have demonstrated that:

1. Educational intervention should begin as early as possible, including home programs;
2. Services should be provided to parents as well as children;
3. Programs should include frequent home visits;
4. Parents should be involved in the instruction of the child, and
5. There should be as few children per teacher as possible. (Consortium for Longitudinal Studies, 1983)

As one reporter of early educational programs for children as young as 2 has noted: It is not a question of whether these programs are effective; it is a matter of providing those programs that are most effective in meeting the developmental needs of children (Perlez, 1986).

Before we discuss the benefits of early reading and the value of children's early experiences with written language, it is important to note that some early childhood teachers vehemently oppose exposing children to print. With some, a sentiment prevails that somehow exposure to print robs young children of their "childhood"; that "children should be allowed to be children"; that adult responsibilities will be forced upon children soon enough. Still others maintain that the child who is pressured toward reading and writing will "block" in his learning, because the exposure to print is unnatural and premature. These fears of some early childhood educators are not entirely unfounded. Parents and teachers who expose very young children to reading by using conventional drill-and-practice procedures may well be producing psychological and educational damage.

For example, a kindergarten teacher who was very much opposed to teaching early reading in the traditional ways (as she should have been) had been coerced by parents and administrators into a phonics-oriented drill-and-practice reading program with her kindergarten class. The children were not succeeding in the overly mechanistic program, and their resistance to the formal lessons contrasted sharply to their enthusiastic behavior during "activity periods," which the teacher did not consider to be language teaching. During activity periods, children were making popcorn snowmen from a recipe, working on a computer program, playing instruments using a large printed song sheet, reading books in the library corner, and doing some invented writing in bird books that they were creating. I said to the teacher, "I don't know what you think you're teaching, but I call it reading—an activity-based reading program. You really aren't getting them to read with that meaningless phonics drill, but everything else is a literacy event." I don't think that she ever really understood that she was teaching reading constantly by encouraging such activities, writing everything down, and exposing children to the literate world around them. Most of the children were reading very well at the end of their year in kindergarten, even though the teacher had abandoned most of her phonics work. The teacher continued to feel that "teaching reading" was poor practice with these children, failing to note that she was, in fact, teaching reading and the children were, in fact, reading. She called her reading program "prereading activity."

In effect, the teacher was engaging in the teaching of reading by creating literacy events, in which she was acting as a mediator. Simply put, she was channeling the interaction of the classroom into print media formats. We can see, using her method as an example, that language, reading, and writing are interactive processes. We live in a literate society, where print and graphic presentations are all around us. The kindergarten teacher in the example above was using, and showing her students different ways to use print and visual formats in the classroom by letting the children explore these forms as they were needed. It is just this kind of "teaching" of reading that is supported in this chapter, and by other authors in this volume.

The very young child knows a great deal about text. The print world is manifest in books, messages, and lists; on packaging, buses, supermarkets, menus, and street signs. Harste et al. (1984) point out just how much the 3-year-old children in their study know:

- Writing serves a pragmatic function, a doing, a social action,
- We placehold thoughts with marks on paper,
- Formation and placement of marks bear a relationship to meaning and conceptual reality,
- Art and writing serve a placeholding function, but they are different from one another,
- Children learn a good deal from encounters with print (storytelling, looking at books, talking about messages in print, etc.). Children are readers and writers long before they begin to form letters and to read print,
- When faced with print, very young children make complex decisions using pragmatics, context of the situation, semantics, syntax, and symbols in a truly sign-semiotic sense. (p. 38)

Children know these facts about language, but not because they are innate readers who learn without being taught. They know about written language, about reading, because they are relating to adults who are mediating between the world of print and the learner's knowledge. These parents, caregivers, and teachers are helping children to see how spoken and written language works through modeling, in transacting with others, by reading and writing themselves, and by helping children to become aware of language and literate environments which are part of their physical and social experience.

Why the rush? Why should print be discussed? Why should children be looking at books or going to the library? Shouldn't we slow things down a bit? The answer is *yes* if children feel pressured and obligated to participate in activities that hold no interest for them. But most children enjoy reading-like activity. When literacy skills are as basic to society as they are to ours, and if the child is willing, then resistance of the parent–teacher–mediator merely holds children back and encourages ignorance. In some ways, it frustrates the child's need for stimulation and retards development of his or her cognitive potential.

Play Activity, Language, and Reading Development

Ideally, reading and writing begin with play. The first picture books, the first messages in print and picture, the first dramatic play—all create worlds that can be managed by the child and that provide opportunities for playing with written language. It is in the world of play that many of the metacognitive strategies may be gained that help the child become aware of his or her environment; playing helps children and their teachers to create literacy events. Play is fun, but also it is a serious activity for the young child, for it enables him or her to work out strategies for his or her social and psychological life. Language development, including some of its written aspects, is part of this created and creative world. The child often makes lists, writes letters, makes signs, reads books, reads magazines, reads advertising, and directions when he or she is playing mother, father, fireman, doctor, nurse, grocer, barber, policeman, teacher, or whatever.

Early reading and writing, including scribbled messages and pictures, should be taken seriously by the teacher. Reading should be correlated with natural activity for the best results. In Heath's (1983) studies of Trackton and Roadville's literate traditions, she found that although both communities were concerned about the literacy of their children, the community that believed literacy was necessary "to be and to do and if reading is necessary for this learning, then reading will occur" was the better developer of children's literacy. The Trackton community seemed to encourage a more active intellectual life and provide for a greater amount of reading in a variety of settings. Roadville residents who practiced the drill-and-practice methods of reading, so it was treated as an instructional lesson, seemed less able to inspire their children with enthusiasm about reading.

What are natural ways that children can be brought to the printed word? Certainly, in a literate society, an awareness that experiences of children and adults can be turned into literacy events is not new, but families and teachers may be unaware of the importance of bringing graphic information to bear in specific situations. Jotting down reminders, making lists, and reading maps, TV guides, newspapers, signs, labels, the junk mail, as well as personal mail, are ways of using everyday situations to foster interest in print. Many practical experiences, such as cooking, shopping, or assembling games, provide opportunities to create graphic information experiences. Pointing out graphic messages as one talks with children is a very viable way of using print to reinforce what is taking place in social settings.

Basic Considerations in Language Development/ Reading Programs

Adults, in social activity with young children, may help children understand graphic messages by pointing out signs and messages, or by writing them and reading them. Whether the adult caregiver is reading books, reading the mail, cooking, talking, taking a walk, reading the paper or a magazine, he or she can use these activities to promote literacy events.

In mediating between a child and print, however, the teacher or parent should consider such factors as the *age*, *maturity*, *interests*, and *willingness* of the child. How interested and ready is the child to talk about, for example, reading the headlines as a part of play activity? Forcing or punishing the child does not encourage a desire for contact with social situations that involve graphic presentations of information. If the young child is not interested or comfortable talking about books and signs, or looking at cereal boxes, pictures, or wordless books, then let the child go on to something else. Children benefit when they are attending and are learning, regardless of whether their immediate experience includes written language.

Finally, whatever learning is taking place and however casual and unplanned it may be, the young child will prosper most in the company of *loving, concerned adults*, who know when to let youngsters explore on their own, play by themselves, watch television and engage in other play for pleasure and for fun. Most helpful is a rich environment for the child to explore with freedom, and sometimes less than more parental and teacher direction about how he or she should learn from this experience is better. Offering too much direction or too much participation can cause the child to withdraw from activity.

Approaches to Early Reading

The Lap Method

A very early approach to books and print is what I call the lap method. From birth, it is natural for parents to hold a child on their laps, to feed and comfort him or her, to enable the infant to participate socially with people around him or her. From this very natural event comes the practice of looking at books. Looking at pictures, telling the story, or reading the story is a very useful way of entertaining a young child, and reading quietly before he or she goes to bed is a reassuring experience. In the beginning, the books may contain only pictures of animals, toys, families, and other familiar things or events; the baby learns to name things in the books. Later, the child learns the rudiments of a story, using perhaps four or five sequenced pictures that relate an event. The parent or caregiver is also learning, to talk with the child about the pictures, about the story, about experiences. These times together can become treasured moments of relating to one another and of caring.

The parent or caregiver may point to words as he or she reads the story or tells about it. Through observation and perhaps by being told, the child learns that each word is separated by spaces from the next, that print goes from left to right and from top to bottom, that the pictures correspond to the print, that there is a way to get messages from print itself, and that this is helpful, interesting and enriching information.

In congenial ways, the child learns how the adult is reading, largely through making sense of the adult's behavior, and shared reading experiences, rather than through direct instruction. The adult can read the sentence; then the child can read it, while the adult points. After a while, quite a good bit of read aloud, read after, and read along activity can occur while pointing to words as the child reads. Sometimes adult and child point together with the adult hand guiding the child's. Sometimes the young child can read pages of one, two, or three words alone. At other times, the child may listen to a tape or a "talking book" while looking and following in the book.

If the child is impatient and does not want to be involved in such ways, then let him or her do as he or she likes with regard to reading.

In time, if "bedtime stories" and other read-aloud experiences with adults are warm, pleasureable, and fun, the child's interest will grow, and a great deal of learning can occur. When reading lapses occur or the young reader misses a beat, it is irrelevant. We learn by doing, by reading, by being involved, so nothing judgmental should occur during this activity—it is simply a way of experiencing print, which is likely to lead to greater familiarity with text. Moreover, the read-aloud, read-along, repeated reading progression is painless. If the child makes a mistake it is not punished and not important—a far different mode from the humiliating round-robin group method and formal instruction in most elementary schools. The assumptions inherent in the natural method of teaching reading allow for personal development in cognition, language and feeling. If the learner does not "pick up" a great deal about the reading process, nothing has been lost, since schooling will occur in any case, but a great deal may have been gained through such practice.

In her studies in New Zealand, Clay (1982) pointed out very wisely that the young child learns to talk by being encouraged. She writes that the child who learns to speak is taught—and fussed over. What he or she says is repeated, encouraged, and praised. Once the child speaks his first word, the expectation is that he or she will learn more words, and the toddler is not corrected or criticized for invented pronunciations. Thus, young children are taught by modeling adult behavior; most adults are clever enough to speak very simply to children, a level above the words that the child is speaking. Adults naturally refrain from using more difficult vocabulary and syntax. Indeed, Clay points out that this is a highly efficacious teaching situation, usually one-to-one, even though the parent or adult who is interacting with the toddler is usually not a licensed teacher, and may not even be aware of "teaching." In the same manner, reading may be taught and learned in natural settings, where children are encouraged, highly regarded, assumed to be successful and praised for their consistent effort. What is appreciated are the children's efforts and achievements.

Gradually, since so much of what we do involves print, the parent may begin to point out words on boxes, packages, frozen foods, and useful items about the house. Parents may provide games and posters that are of interest to the child, as well as clay, crayons, magic markers, pencils, paints, and other materials that the child can use to make pictures, to write messages or letters, to make alphabet letters, to write his or her name. Children's experiments with graphic representation can occur very early, although they may not have much meaning at first (indeed, these efforts seem like scribbling or designs), but the child learns more about language with each experience.

Creating literacy from basic experience, we move naturally into the world of books themselves. There are many attractive books for children that are plastic and indestructible, and easy to understand with only pictures or pictures combined with a few words. Activities can be devised by parents who want to make reading fun: creating puzzles, rhymes, notes, posters, mazes, letters, and participating in songs and chants. Putting labels around the house and in the child's room, or leaving notes and mail for the child can delight and stimulate children, and increase their interest in written language, often leading children to emulate some of the activities of adults.

Finally, there are many stimulating and educational programs for children on television. Many of these, such as *Sesame Street*, *Mr. Rogers Neighborhood*, and the *Electric Company*, directly promote reading and language activity. Children get most from these programs when they can talk about them with adults. If the youngster is to get the most from television, he or she should be encouraged to look things up in the TV guide. Children usually do not take long to recognize the names of their favorite programs, or to tell what time they air by using digital clocks.

In summary, the lap method includes:

- Holding the child and talking about books, pictures, experiences, and things; getting the plot and the sequence of events,
- Reading aloud and pointing to print, or
- Reading along with the child, "saying it with Mother," while still pointing to the printed words, preferably together,
- Reading-after or repeated readings. The child reads the sentence after mother or teacher.
- Extending this method to any practical literacy activity, such as reading recipes, junk mail, or letters.

Creating Literacy through Writing

Thus far, we have talked about written language in the receptive mode—that is, reading. What about methods that include reading as a part of writing? Many feel that this is a first way of learning about the written word. Studies show that reading and writing evolve as a gradual part of socialization in a literate society, rather than from acts of direct teaching (Clay, 1982; Cochran–Smith, 1984). Such is the position advocated in this chapter. Print is interwoven into the social fabric of everyday life. As part of everyday situations, we write lists, telephone messages, letters, and generally make print a part of our living and being. Children likewise can create; as we talk with children, we (and they) can make notes, lists, or posters, write down their thoughts, make scrapbooks, and make books dictated by children and/or created from magazines. The underlying philosophy is that what can be talked about can be written down, and that what is written down can be preserved and read by the child and by others.

A child's mailbox, where an adult leaves written messages, perhaps including photographs, is a way of fostering writing. Later, the child can write messages in response, using pictures and invented writing. Adults may find it helpful to congratulate the writer on his or her work, however "primitive" it may be. Let the youngster read the letter, tell about it, ask for things in writing. No matter that these first beginnings seem like scribbling; writing will change, letters will be formed, invented spellings and pictures will sharpen the presentation. The adult may help when invited, or when interaction is part of the event, but negative comments and corrections should be avoided. Thus, the caregiver models writing behaviors and gives help if the child seeks guidance.

In the preschool setting, where writing is one of the literacy events sponsored by the school, the teacher can write a "story" dictated by the child, using a picture or painting or a creative work by the child to initiate the writing experience. Stories about home, feelings, pets, or any other topic which is within the experiential or fantasy life of the child may be created together. These topical books can be read in class. Short rhymes and other forms of short word stories in which the child uses his or her own vocabulary can be developed. Some schools are introducing ways for children to write on computers, using simple word-processing programs. Many of these computer programs enable the child to format, to write legibly, and to correct spelling, which may be a boon for those children who become self-conscious if papers don't "look nice."

In short, young children are virtually surrounded with print in a literate society; much of this graphic language or print can be of their own creation. Children should be appreciated for their authorship, and their work should be read, so that what they have created generates a response. As an important component of an environment that informs children, print cannot be ignored; it is part of what caregiving adults talk about, especially if that print has been created by the children themselves. The teacher as mediator between child and print is as important in the creation of print (writing) as in the discovery of print (reading).

The Mechanics of Reading and Writing

What do we want young children to know about word analysis? Using natural methods of exposure to the graphic aspect of language, should we adhere to whole language and meaning or concern ourselves with aspects of decoding? These are controversial issues that merit discussion.

Within the whole language framework, meaning is a first concern. Concepts of letter recognition, sight words, letter sounds, sound–symbol relationships, breaking words into parts, should follow from meaningful reading. Learning such concepts is beyond the ability of most children in preschool or kindergarten. However, most will want to learn some letters, at least those in their name or on street signs. Alphabet books, most of them delightful, are commonplace. Alphabet strips can be put in the child's room as reference materials near a writing table. Thus when the learner wants to write, he or she can easily look up some letters. Reading aloud or writing, the child may find that he or she cannot read or spell some of the words. It is all right for caregivers to show that letters stand for sounds, that words can be sounded out. Clay (1986) advises that phonics instruction be given while writing; as the child writes he or she pronounces the sound that the letter stands for as he writes it. Such practice results in the invented spellings of the interpreted phonic system, but the principle of sound–symbol relationship is firmly established. Clay advocates a progression of word analysis events flowing from natural reading of children's books:

- Make sure that the child can hear a distinction or difference between the two sounds or two words before you teach him or her to *see* the difference.
- Start with large units of meaning, not small ones: Separate words out of phrases, separate letters out of words.
- Encourage the use of the eye and hand together; eyes-alone reading occurs later in the learning sequence.
- Link something the child does easily with something he or she finds hard, before asking for the difficult response.
- Teach by demonstration and by modeling. Use questioning only for established responses.
- Try to teach a few items (letters, words, sounds) and then try to establish further examples by strategies of comparison. The child needs to know a few items and a few strategies for picking up new techniques later as he or she reads.
- Try to teach the child to be independent, self-improving; try to see how one comes to know. "How did you know that?"

Thus, on a need to know basis, children, even very young ones, can learn some word identification techniques, letter identification, letter sounds (especially the consonants, which seem to be more hearable), a little phonics or sounding out, a little rhyming, a few sight words (not the Dolch list, but many of those words from daily experience and the world of advertising), and a few of the word families (cat, rat, fat, etc.). The young child is learning and print can help in cognitive achievement; the more the child learns about the system of graphic language, the better for his or her educational future.

Parenting and Home Environments for Literacy

Parental involvement is critical if children, particularly young children, are to prosper in the educational environment. Yet we no longer live in an age where the concept of the nuclear family holds. In the family of today, both parents may work; they may try to provide quality time and weekends for their children, but more and more of the care of young children is provided by schools and child-care centers. Many other children live in single-parent families in which the one parent is working and often fatigued. In some cases, children rotate between two households; there are also shared parents, stepparents, and extended family parents, where the children are not cared for by their natural parents at all. Not only may these conditions be confusing for the child, but parents involved in these situations are not bringing up their children as they were brought up; therefore, much of what is happening is experimental, haphazard, and unproven. We are in the process of constructing new and different kinds of child care; new educational systems must be devised that will meet changing educational and social needs. Whatever the outcome from this generation's child-rearing practices, much of it will not be negative, despite the laments of many of the experts.

In fact, there are many positive aspects to current trends in child rearing. First, fewer children are brought into the world who are not wanted, due to advanced methods of birth control. Further, the birth of children is often postponed until some of the parents' needs are fulfilled; frequently today's parents are more educated or more experienced when they have children than were parents in the past. Third, there are fewer children per family, which may mean that they have more educational "things," more stimulation, better care and more involvement with their parents. Another boon to child rearing in our time is television. Programs with advice about child rearing abound, and many of them are enlightened, informing parents as to how to socialize their young and how to educate them comfortably. Finally, the environment in which children are brought up may be far more stimulating:

Television, computers, telephone access systems, videocassettes, microwave cookery and countless other technologies are bringing the world into our homes in ways that were not dreamed of, even 25 years ago.

These factors are conducive to better teacher–parent interaction. Working parents who pick up their children from school are more prone to talk with the teachers, more apt to know about the life of the school and are more understanding of the fact that the home and the care center are going to have to work closely in bringing up the child. The school can capitalize on this parental involvement. Parents must help to create literacy environments in ways, such as those listed above, that are fun and foolproof in terms of preventing children's failure in the socialization and literacy process. Simply interacting with the child in ways which acknowledge the value of the word in print form adds to interaction and fun. In painlessly effective ways, children learn to love a world which they can manage better and which is richer because print is part of it.

Children and Frustration with Reading

What causes children to see themselves as failures at reading? What turns them off? What frustrates them when reading? Angers them? Causes them to value themselves less? Clearly, a great deal of individual trauma can occur when learning to read. When we know so much about positive reading experiences, which can begin at virtually any age level with interaction with young children, how do we go wrong in our teaching? If the child is unwilling to do the task, then it may be *too hard*. The early reading experiences described above are not a mandatory or even a desired exercise if the child is *unwilling*. Time and maturity will take care of interest and reading discovery. If material does not build on the *interest* of the child, if the youngster is fretful and inattentive, parents or caregivers should go on to something that the child wants to do. Interests are infectious; if the adult is interested and is modeling behavior which reflects that interest, then often the child becomes interested—but on his own terms.

An adult can spend *too much time* on a literacy event that involves print. Two minutes may be optimum in talking about a book or pictures. In sharing one's life with a child, it is possible to be too formal, too rigid, and too anxious in trying to turn experience into literacy acts. In other words, the caregiving adult becomes unnatural in structuring events, turning the interaction into instruction and *regimentation*. Thus in some ways, the interaction has some of the characteristics of formal reading instruction, for adults are no longer sharing an experience in a social way, rather they are demanding that the child learn. Educators are understanding more and more that when teachers and parents do not build on what a child thinks and says, when they are being didactic, their behavior frustrates learning. We do better to provide the learner with models of socialized behavior, where he or she is accepted as a participant in social activities that are not divorced from the adult world, which includes print.

Do children *understand* what they are reading? Adults can query children and accept their explanations. Probe more deeply, but do not reject or correct their interpretation of a language event, which is valid in terms of their cognitive ability and their experience. Children are not adults. One must listen to know how to respond. When we are overcome with the need to impart information—in this case, a familiarity with the print world—we are no longer in a position to, in fact, teach.

Having Fun with Reading and Writing

Having taken the position that parents, caregivers, and teachers are working together to create literacy events, one cannot fail to note that stimulating environments should include new experiences. The child in school, the teacher doing a job, the parent who is working—all need a respite from daily activities in familiar settings. Children should help plan vacations, read the maps, read the travel guides and the camping literature; they may want to write diaries or make pictures of yesterday's outing or picnic. In learning crafts—pottery, leather, macrame, weaving, woodcarving, woodburning—children may use models, rebus materials, pictures, and graphics. By the same token, becoming a collector demands a knowledge of the dimensions of the job, whether collecting coins, comics, barbed wire, or bottles.

Reference materials are an important component of an instant gratification, do-it-yourself, high-technology culture. The computer may be able to do everything including play games with the bored youngster, but only if he or she is computer literate and able to read about the game being played. Children whose parents rent videocassettes and tapes must learn how to use the catalog and the files. For the evening at home, a movie, microwave popcorn and soft drinks can be provided, along with a meal put together using convenience foods. But only if you are a reader! The microwave directions must be read, the popcorn box must be read, and the potatoes must be prepared by following directions.

As we move more rapidly into a high-technology era, there is little evidence that community is breaking down; the nuclear family and its reading habits may be changing, but the need and demand for community was never greater. Children refuse to be bored; they know the future is waiting, but only if they can exercise a little control over this fast-paced universe by becoming literate at many levels and by using symbols in new and inventive ways. Given the world that we expect children to inherit, we are right to expect more from this generation. Literacy may be redefined by the fourth level of technology that is upon us, but it can never be ignored.

References

Anderson, J. R., Osborn, J., & Tierney, R. J. (1984). *Learning to read in American schools.* Hillsdale, NJ: Erlbaum.

Applebee, A. N. (1978). *The child's concept of story.* University of Chicago Press.

Clay, M. M. (1982). *Observing young readers.* Portsmouth, NH: Heinemann.

Clay, M. M. (1985). *The early detection of reading difficulties* (3rd ed.). Portsmouth, NH: Heinemann.

Cochran–Smith, M. (1984). *The making of a reader.* Norwood, NJ: Ablex Publishing.

Collins, J. L. (1983). *Teaching all the children to write.* Buffalo, NY: New York State English Council.

Consortium for Longitudinal Studies. (1983). *As the twig is bent: Lasting effects of preschool programs.* Hillsdale, NJ: Erlbaum.

Durkin, D. (1982). *Getting reading started.* Boston: Allyn & Bacon.

Durkin, D. (1985). *Teaching young children to read.* Boston: Allyn & Bacon.

Ferreiro, E., & Teberosky, A. (1982). *Literacy before schooling.* Portsmouth, NH: Heinemann.

Fletcher, P. (1985). *A child's learning of English.* Oxford, England: Basil Blackwell.

Garvey, C. (1977). *Play.* Cambridge, MA: Harvard University Press.

Genishi, C., & Dyson, A. H. (1984). *Language assessment in the early years.* Norwood, NJ: Ablex Publishing.

Glazer, S. M. (1980). *Getting ready to read.* Englewood Cliffs, NJ: Prentice–Hall.

Goelman, H., Oberg, A., & Smith, F. (1984). *Awakening to literacy.* Portsmouth, NH: Heinemann.

Goodlad, J. (1983). *A study of schooling.* New York: McGraw–Hill.

Hardt, U. H. (1983). *Teaching reading with the other language arts.* Newark, DE: International Reading Association.

Harms, J. M. (1982). *Comprehension and literature.* Dubuque, IA: Kendall Hunt.

Harste, J., Woodward, V., & Burke, C. (1984). *Language stories and literacy lessons.* Portsmouth, NH: Heinemann.

Heath, S. (1983). *Ways with words.* New York: Cambridge University Press.

Hedley, C. N., & Baratta, A. N. (1985). *Contexts of reading.* Norwood, NJ: Ablex Publishing.

Holdaway, D. (1983). *Stability and change in literacy learning*. London: Heinemann.

Johnson, D. D., & Pearson, P. D. (1985). *Teaching reading vocabulary*. New York: Holt, Rinehart, & Winston.

Kaye, P. (1984). *Games for reading: Playful ways to help your child read*. New York: Pantheon Books.

McNeil, J. D. (1984). *Reading comprehension*. Glenview, IL: Scott Foresman.

Newman, J. M. (1985). *Whole language: Theory in use*. Portsmouth, NH: Heinemann.

Pearson, P. D., & Johnson, D. D. (1986). *Teaching reading comprehension*. New York: Holt, Rinehart, & Winston.

Perera, K. (1984). *Children's writing and reading: Analysing classroom language*. Oxford, England: Basil Blackwell.

Perlez, J. (1986, July 24). City will begin schooling plan for 4-year-olds. *New York Times*, sec. 2, p. 1.

Potter, G. (1986). Early literacy development—It's time to align the curriculum with children's developmental stages. *The Reading Teacher, 39*, 628–631.

Smith, F. (1983). *Essays into literacy*. Portsmouth, NH: Heinemann.

Stewig, J. W. (1982). *Teaching language arts in early childhood*. New York: Holt, Rinehart, & Winston.

Taylor, D. (1983). *Family literacy*. Portsmouth, NH: Heinemann.

Temple, C. A., Nathan, R. G., & Burris, N. A. (1979). *The beginnings of writing*. Boston: Allyn & Bacon.

Tierney, R. J., Readence, J. E., & Dishner, E. K. (1985). *Reading strategies and practices* (2nd ed.). Boston: Allyn & Bacon.

Tough, J. (1976). *Listening to children talking*. London: Ward Lock Educational.

Tough, J. (1977). *Talking and learning*. London: Ward Lock Educational.

Tucker, N. (1981). *The child and the book*. Cambridge, England: Cambridge University Press.

Vygotsky, L. S. (1978). *Mind in society*. Cambridge, MA: Harvard University Press.

Wells, G. (1981). *Learning through interaction: A study in language development*. Cambridge, England: Cambridge University Press.

Wells, G. (1986). *The meaning makers: Children learning language and using language to learn*. Portsmouth, NH: Heinemann.

Yaden, D. B., & Templeton, S. (1986). *Metalinguistic awareness and beginning literacy*. Portsmouth, NH: Heinemann.

Chapter 5

The Language of Social Regulation in Young Children

Emily Comstock DiMartino

Fordham University

Story 1

Billy and Nick are first graders who are sitting on the floor of the classroom playing with blocks. Each boy has made an elaborate reconstruction of the apartment building in which he lives. Nick gets up to go over to the teacher and ask for some paper and a pencil to label his structure. While he is gone, Billy moves closer to Nicky's building and knocks it down. Nick returns, saying, "Hey. That was my building and you ruined it." Billy responds, "Oh. Come on. You can make another one, see."

Story 2

Sara and Jennifer, both 6 years old, are watching TV at Jennifer's house. During the commercial break, Sara gets up, goes to the kitchen and helps herself to some cheese bits and fruit that are in the refrigerator. She returns to the living room, carrying the remaining pieces of cheese in her hand. Jennifer says, "Hey, you're not supposed to take food from the refrigerator without asking me first." Sara responds, "Well, it's almost gone now."

Story 3

Dan and Joe are playing on the slide in the playground. After many trips down the slide in a seated position, Joe, who is standing at the top of the slide, starts to run down the slide. He makes it safely down, falling only after he hits the bottom of the slide. Two teachers stop what they're doing and come over. As Joe gets up, one teacher says,

"Joe, that is not a safe thing to do. The slide must be used sitting down and that's what I want you to do."

Story 4

Every day a "line leader" is chosen for the day. At lunch time this child gets to be first on line for the cafeteria. It is lunch time and Karen, who is not the line leader for the day, stands at the head of the line. Barbara yells, "Hey, Karen, only the leader gets to be at the head of the line and you're not the leader today."

The children in these stories are participating in some of the many social regulatory episodes or breaches which occur during the course of a child's day, at home, at school, in the play yard; anywhere, in fact, where more than one child is found. Can these children, in fact, differentiate between those social conflicts which involve a moral issue (harm or injustice—Story 1) from those dilemmas involving manners (Story 2), safety (Story 3), or organizational rules (Story 4)? If they do treat different kinds of social breaches in different ways, is the manner in which children interpret and carry out their role as social actors similar to that of adults? Do young girls respond to social breaches like young boys? Or are their responses more closely allied with those of adult females and the boys' with those of adult males?

Underlying all of these questions is a more basic one: Is social cognitive understanding principally a developmental phenomenon? Is an understanding of others a matter of restructuring what one knows into systems of meaning or belief? Does what one learns from experience depend heavily on how one structures those experiences? Following this line of thought, age then would be a critical variable in understanding children's social knowledge. The concept of developmental stages is contingent upon the natural unfolding of structures as the child interacts with the environment.

Perhaps there is another approach to understanding children's active participation in and resolution of social conflicts. Perhaps children's social cognitive understanding is not a developmental issue at all. Persons in social situations may act and react based upon their own internal states and upon the significant social cues provided by the other participants. Nisbett, Borgida, Crandall, and Reed (1976) have indicated that in social interactions, intuitive, rather than information-processing, strategies are more commonly used and they are most likely to be spurred by tacit knowledge. Shweder (1982) noted that children's ability to understand social regulatory transactions occurs naturally as a result of living within a given social environment. Tentative answers to these and other questions lie ahead.

What Is Social Regulation?

What is social regulation? Social regulation refers simply to those situations where it is legitimate to mind other people's business and to regulate other people's behavior. Conduct subject to social regulation includes that which is harmful to another or unjust (a moral issue as in Story 1); unconventional or impolite (a question of manners or custom as in Story 2); dangerous (Story 3); and not allowed (an issue involving a specific institutional rule, e.g., a classroom rule as in Story 4). It is through an analysis of the language that young children use to convey their understanding and resolution of social conflicts that researchers are able to discern the extent to which children are able to differentiate cognitively between these acts in the same way as adults.

Cognitive differentiation refers to the degree to which domains of knowledge or discourse are distinguished. In social cognitive development, cognitive differentiation involves the extent to which children and adults distinguish among the variety of social regulatory transactions which take place in everyday living (Shweder, 1982). Many scholars, most notably Piaget (1970) and Kohlberg (1969, 1973), have portrayed young children as unable to differentiate social cognitive issues because they confound rational or moral forms of evaluating social episodes with conventional forms. Piaget, for example, characterized the young child as regarding right and wrong in an absolute way. The authoritarian quality of this absolutism is suggested in Piaget's (1932, 1965) finding that young children tend to judge rules set down by adults as good, while any act which does not conform to these rules is considered bad. Stages 1 and 2 in his moral developmental paradigm can be termed the "morality of physical absolutes" and "the morality of instrumental exchange," respectively, with the child first viewing rules as sacred and immutable, much like physical laws, then subsequently seeing rules as protecting his interest in interpersonal contexts. It is in the third moral stage, which emerges as the child approaches adolescence, that rational issues are seen as different from and superior to conventional and pragmatic issues.

Kohlberg (1969, 1973) elaborated on Piaget's first three stages of moral development while adding three new ones. Stages 1 and 2 are called preconventional morality as social issues are evaluated based on prudential considerations. Conventional morality appears during stages 3 and 4 in which conformity and maintenance of the rules of society serve as guides for conduct in social situations. Stages 5 and 6 in the Kohlbergian model are postconventional and emerge as the individual displaces prudential and conventional concerns with an ideal or principled approach to interpreting social events. Thus, for Piaget and Kohlberg, cognitive differentiation of social regulatory transactions occurs gradually as the growing child passes through the stages of development. The child may or may not reach the most advanced developmental stages where clear distinctions between convention, prudence, and morality are made.

Studies carried out by Pool, Shweder and Much (1980) and DiMartino (1985) have indicated that children are able to differentiate among moral, conventional, and prudential issues at a far younger age than that posited by Piaget and Kohlberg. Preschoolers appear to understand and separate rule types using the same formal criteria of validity employed by adults, namely: prescriptively, what ought to be; obligation, duty; and importance, extent to which a rule is considered serious (Pool, Shweder, & Much, 1980).

When working with children between the ages of 3 and 8, the more formal reading of a dilemma followed by a series of interview questions or probes is less age-appropriate than it might be for the older populations studied by Kohlberg. Instead, researchers such as Nucci, Shweder, and DiMartino have examined the language and images young children use when dealing with the many breach episodes or transgressions that children encounter. Social conflicts offer a large window to view the social world of the child. It is through reactions to cultural breaches and attempts to repair them that social actors, old and young, convey a great deal of information regarding the basis for particular social and moral standards. With children, in particular, it may be a case of knowing more than they can tell. What may appear to a researcher as a child's lack of social cognitive understanding may, in fact, be a failure of his methodology to retrieve that child's knowledge (Shultz, Wright, & Schleifer, 1986).

As Much and Shweder (1978) and later Shweder, Turiel, and Much (1980) discovered, the kinds of accounts given by children differentiate rational or moral issues from conventional and safety ones. the children, for example, in episodes involving moral breaches made reference to the intrinsic wrongness of the act or simply denied that the act occurred. No reference was made to school rules or conventions, nor was the teacher called upon to intervene. In fact, when asked if it would be all right to commit some act that would hurt another child if there were no rule, the children invariably answered, "No," indicating the unalterable nature of a moral issue. Conventional and school rule violations, on the other hand, provoked numerous references by the children to circumstances and conditions which might alter the rule and made many requests for teacher intervention. According to these researchers, this difference in children's responses to episodes involving social transgressions indicates a perception of moral or rational issues as prescriptive and beyond negotiation or rules. Conventional issues and school rules are, conversely, subject to consequences, exceptions, and adult interpretation.

Nucci and Turiel (1980) asked preschool children and adults to evaluate a set of 72 breach episodes derived from earlier observations. The children were required to respond to the question, "What if there weren't a rule in the school about (the observed situation); would it be all right to do it then?" This query addressed the unalterable nature of moral issues as opposed to the relative or situationally dependent nature of conventional and school rules. Adults were requested to categorize the episodes as moral or conventional, employing similar definitions of the two domains. Eighty-three percent of the time the preschoolers and adults responded alike, with the children answering "yes" to those questions about social events that the adults listed as conventional and "no" to those which were regarded as rational or moral in nature.

Nucci (1981) reported a series of five observational studies of social interactions revolving around cultural breaches and the efforts made to repair them by preschool teachers and children in the United States and the Virgin Islands in free-play settings. Nucci found that morality and convention made up aspects of separate conceptual and developmental domains.

> In particular, the findings indicate that social interactions in the context of moral events stem from the intrinsic features of acts as they affect the rights and well-being of others, while interactions in the context of conventions focus on the aspects of the social order. (p. 1)

Recently DiMartino (1985), using episodes similar to the four stories presented at the beginning of this chapter, studied the degree to which children ages 7½ to 8½ and adults are differentiated in their modes of applying adjectives of appraisal to social transgressions. The purpose of this study was to determine if children were able to distinguish between moral, conventional, safety, and school rules in the same manner as adults. If children and adults made similar distinctions among the episodes, then it would indicate that perhaps social cognitive understandings are not strictly developmental in nature and thus only completely within the grasp of the adult, but might be available also to very young children via social-cultural transmission.

Any cultural environment is laden with implicit and explicit messages about what is important, who is important, what things mean and so on, and these messages are acted upon in a similar manner by children and adults. This tacit knowledge forms an unseen network existent in any social environment which provides coherence to social exchanges.

It is knowledge that is not self-constructed by the child as he or she interacts with his environment but rather is socially constructed. Socially constructed knowledge is not figured out by the child. It is received knowledge, according to D'Andrade (1981), transmitted from parent to child, teacher to child, child to child.

Investigating children's everyday language through observation studies, interview probes, and questionnaires, DiMartino (1985) determined that children and adults are different in their appraisals of breach episodes, but that children appear more able to differentiate appropriately the various social regulatory stories than do the adults. That is, the younger subjects showed greater accuracy than did the adults in evaluating which stories involve moral dilemmas and which involve safety or issues of prudence. What is the reason for the children's greater ability to differentiate moral breaches from conventional, prudential, and school-rule social breaches? The answer may lie in the fact that the child's concepts of right and wrong tend to be more (not less) precise, more unequivocal, even monolithic. When evaluating the moral dilemmas, for example, the children were clear and unidimensional in their assessments of the behavior of the child in the breach episode in the story. The adults also would apply terms of moral condemnation when evaluating the misconduct of the child in the story but they, in addition, applied terms from the conventional domain, such as bad manners, good manners, and acceptable, demonstrating a broader interpretation of the story. As adults they have had more complex experiences and relationships than the children and this may lead to a more diffuse, more complex interpretation of social interactions.

Very young children appear to have an intuitive ability to partition social regulation into subcategories of harm, convention, good sense, and school rules in the same manner as adults. Most of the basic conceptual structures of moral reasoning are in place by age 5, according to Shultz et al. (1986). It seems, as stated by D'Andrade (1981), Glick (1978), and Shweder (1982) that social rule understandings are carried within the socialization process of the culture. By the time they enter kindergarten, children have received many of the society's messages concerning behavior in social regulatory situations. As they grow older and have more varied experiences and relationships, their social understanding likely becomes broader and less unidimensional. According to this theory, regular changes over time in children's social judgments reflect the changing modeling and reinforcement contingencies of the social environment. These changes are not age-bound but rather occur concomitantly with the variation of actors and cues in social situations (Bandura, 1977; D'Andrade, 1981; Glick, 1978; Shweder, 1982).

The results of this research contrast sharply to the cognitive developmental psychologists who maintain that social rule understandings are self-constructed by the child as he grows, and that only as the child reaches maturity can he differentiate among the various kinds of social conflicts he encounters. However, current research is demonstrating that when the language of social interaction is analyzed, children have a very clear sense of what is happening as they cope with the many social breaches or conflicts in their daily lives.

In addition to comparing and contrasting the everyday language of children with that of adults in order to retrieve information on children's understanding of the many social conflicts in which they are often the central characters, studying the differences in the language and images of males and females, both young and old, also yields insights into how young children understand their social world. To derive research criteria from the language of everyday social regulatory discourse, it is necessary first to see if female construction of social rule understandings relies on a different form of expression than that of males.

Developmental researchers (Bar–Yam, 1980; Edwards, 1981; Holstein, 1976; Kohlberg, 1981) have claimed universality for their stage sequence of moral development, and yet girls, when studied, frequently fail to reach the higher stages. Gender comparisons have been made on the basis of the age-stage progression using models (a) that are derived from the study of male social interaction and (b) that assume a cognitive developmental approach to the understanding of social knowledge.

Sex Differences

Baumrind (1986), Gilligan (1982), and Lyons (1985) have all reported findings that indicate that there are sex differences in moral reasoning. Gilligan and Lyons posit that boys apply logical thinking to moral dilemmas, yielding what these researchers term a "morality of fair" based on rights and rules. Girls, on the other hand, repeatedly stress communication, responsibility, and relationships when resolving moral issues, which is called a "morality of care." The contrasting language and images in boys' and girls' discussions of social regulatory issues provide, according to this interpretation, two approaches to morality which are complementary, not sequential or opposed, and which are the result of early experiences and tacit messages pervasive in the social environment. It is not the intent in this chapter to analyze genetic differences between males and females as a contributive factor to understanding how social cognitive information is processed. It must be noted here, though, that the socialization process for young male and female children is laden with overt and covert gender role definition messages which very likely promote differences in the way boys and girls resolve conflicts.

DiMartino (1985) found that females were as able to distinguish moral issues from other kinds of social regulatory situations subject to the instruments used to evaluate them. In addition, DiMartino reported that females were able to combine the ability to empathize with the feelings and experiences of others, that is, how one would feel if it happened to him or her, with a logical analysis of the problem. This interpersonal logic of the female subjects was demonstrated in an analysis by sex of the language used to discuss social breaches similar in nature to the examples given at the start of the chapter.

First, as might be expected, greater use of projecting language was demonstrated by the females, both young and old, projecting both into the feelings and experiences of others. Second, once they had taken the other's point of view, the females would use a great many more if-then statements based on logic involving human feelings and experiences. Statements made by the females always stressed the importance of the conditional interpretation when discussing human social interactions. Perhaps this is best illustrated by the responses of an 8-year-old girl to the interview question following the reading of a story in which one young girl had just torn up the painting of another young girl. When queried, what would you do if you saw someone tearing up someone else's drawing, she replied,

> Well, it would depend. If it happened that a few days ago the other girl had hit her or something that would be one thing. If the girl was jealous of the other girl's picture that would be another. If she was just in a bad mood that would be even another thing. I don't know what I would do; it would just depend.

This application of interpersonal logic to social breach episodes indicates that this young female subject was able to project into the conditions under which the social transgression might have occurred and also was able to provide a reasoned or logical analysis of the possible effects of these conditions on the behavior of the participants involved. This was not an atypical female response, but rather a common one. Perhaps then, this desire for understanding and continuity in social interactions is based not only on strong female empathetic and nurturant behaviors but also on a sophisticated application of interpersonal logic which would promote the continuance of the relationship should a breach arise but which could also lead to ambiguity and indecisiveness. Let's save these last two issues for another day.

The males in the DiMartino study used the language and logic of common sense and rules to decide appropriate responses to school transgressions. If the issue involved danger, the males, young and old, used common sense as their guide. If the issue involved morality or manners, then invariably the males made reference to some person, rule, or regulation that would arbitrate or resolve the issue. This type of thinking demonstrated less tolerance for ambiguity and less appreciation for the variety of circumstances under which a social transaction may have occurred but it did provide quicker, more straightforward decision making. For example, in the same episode involving the young girl who tore up another girl's drawing, a typical boy's response went like this:

Interviewer: *What would you do if you saw a person doing something like this?*

Boy: *I would tell the person to stop and I would also tell the teacher.*

Not one young male interviewee made reference to the circumstances or conditions which might have had an impact on the behavior in question. Each boy dealt simply and directly with stopping the misconduct and did not appear interested in the reasons for the misdeed.

But what does it all mean? How does it help the classroom teacher to know that her 4-year-olds are quite savvy to what is happening during the course of the many, many social conflicts that they are involved in and that she must arbitrate? Does it really matter that there may well be systematic differences in the ways that boys and girls approach social dilemmas?

A primary concern of practitioners in education is a need for increased adult credibility when communicating with young children. If educators are aware that very young children can and do distinguish acts which carry intrinsic merit from acts which are conventional or society-bound, then teacher directives can be modified to suit the importance of the acts. Teachers who use the same language and tone in situations involving harm to another child and in those pertaining to dress or manner of sitting in a chair run the risk of losing credibility with their audience. Furthermore, parents are increasingly requesting that schools take a more active role in the teaching of ethics, values, and social understanding (Pietig, 1983). Research and information on the domains of social knowledge and on the variations among people in the extent and kinds of differentiation of rule understandings will enable formulators of the direct and indirect values curriculum to clarify their goals and objectives for instruction.

Preschool and very young school-age children are not too young to appreciate and evaluate complex social interactions which are a major part of their daily routines. The different approaches applied by boys as opposed to girls to assess and respond to social breach episodes, especially those involving moral issues, should be noted by the professional staff and employed by them to increase understanding between the groups. Projecting into the feelings and experiences of others, interpersonal logic, tolerance of ambiguity and the ability to make decisions are all issues which are affected by the child's social cognitive understanding. And through what they say and what they do all young children communicate their extensive social knowledge and its application to the world around them.

References

Bandura, A. (1977). *Social learning theory*. Englewood Cliffs, NJ: Prentice-Hall.

Bar–Yam, M. (1980). Moral reasoning of students in the different cultural, social, and educational settings. *American Journal of Education, 88,* 345–362.

Baumrind, D. (1986). Sex differences in moral reasoning: Response to Walker's (1984) conclusion that there are none. *Child Development, 57,* 511–521.

D'Andrade, R. G. (1981). The cultural part of cognition. *Cognitive Science, 42,* 179–195.

DiMartino, E. C. (1985). *The relationship between age, sex and the language of social regulation*. Doctoral dissertation, Fordham University, New York.

Edwards, C. P. (1981). The comparative study of the development of moral judgment and reasoning. In R. H. Munroe, R. L. Munroe, & B. Whiting (Eds.), *Handbook of cross-cultural human development* (pp. 501–530). New York: Garland Press.

Gilligan, C. (1982). *In a different voice*. Cambridge, MA: Harvard University Press.

Glick, J. (1978). Cognition and social cognition: An introduction. In J. Glick & A. Clarke–Stewart (Eds.), *The development of social understanding* (pp. 1–10). New York: Gardner Press.

Holstein, C. (1976). Development of moral judgment: A longitudinal study of males and females. *Child Development, 47,* 51–61.

Kohlberg, L. (1969). Stage and sequence: The cognitive–developmental approach to socialization. In D. A. Goslin (Ed.), *Handbook of socialization theory and research* (pp. 347–480). Chicago: Rand McNally.

Kohlberg, L. (1973). Continuities in childhood and adult moral development revisited. In P. B. Baltes & L. R. Goulet (Eds.), *Life-span developmental psychology* (2nd ed., pp. 126–149). New York: Academic Press.

Kohlberg, L. (1981). *The philosophy of moral development*. San Francisco: Harper & Row.

Kohlberg, L., & Kramer, R. (1969). Continuities and discontinuities in child and adult moral development. *Human Development, 12,* 93–120.

Lyons, N. (1985). *Male and female moral development.* Unpublished presentation at Fordham University, New York.

Much, N. C., & Shweder, R. A. (1978). Speaking of rules: The analysis of culture in breach. In W. Damon (Ed.), *New directions for child development: Moral development* (pp. 24–49). San Francisco: Jossey-Bass.

Murphy, J. M., & Gilligan, C. (1980). Moral development in late adolescence and adulthood: A critique and reconstruction of Kohlberg's theory. *Human Development, 23,* 77–104.

Nisbett, R. E., Borgida, E., Crandall, R., & Reed, H. (1976). Popular induction. In J. S. Carroll & J. W. Payne (Eds.), *Cognition and social behavior* (pp. 122–159). Hillsdale, NJ: Erlbaum.

Nucci, L. P. (1981, April). *Forms of social interaction and the domains of social understanding.* Paper presented at the biennial meeting of the Society for Research in Child Development, Boston.

Nucci, L. P., & Turiel E. (1980). Social interactions and the development of social concepts in pre-school children. *Child Development, 49,* 400–407.

Piaget, J. (1965). *The moral judgment of the child.* New York: Free Press. (Originally published 1932)

Piaget, J. (1970). Piaget's theory. In P. Mussen (Ed.), *Carmichael's handbook of child psychology* (pp. 8–29). New York: Wiley.

Pietig, J. (1983). Values and morality in early twentieth century schools: A perspective. *Social Education, 45,* 262–265.

Pool, D. L., Shweder, R. A., & Much, N. C. (1980). Culture as a cognitive system: Differentiated role understandings in children and other savages. In E. T. Higgins, D. H. Rable, & W. W. Mallup (Eds.), *Social cognition and social behavior: Developmental perspectives* (pp. 112–188). San Francisco: Jossey-Bass.

Shultz, T. R., Wright, K., & Schleifer, M. (1986). Assignment of moral responsibility and punishment. *Child Development, 57,* 177–184.

Shweder, R. A. (1982). Beyond self-constructed knowledge: The study of culture and morality. *Merrill Palmer Quarterly, 28,* 41–70.

Shweder, R. A., Turiel, E., & Much, N. C. (1980). In L. Ross & J. Havell (Eds.), *New directions in the study of social-cognitive development* (pp. 71–98). New York: Cambridge University Press.

Walker, L. J. (1986). Sex differences in the development of moral reasoning: A rejoinder to Baumrind. *Child Development, 57,* 522–526.

Chapter 6

The (Con)Textual Worlds of Childhood: An Interpretive Approach to Alternative Dimensions of Experience

Denny Taylor

Teachers College, Columbia University

Young Peter, who is just 3, lives in a house with eyebrow dormers over the windows. The house is on a dirt road that is closed in the mud season. It is surrounded by meadows, trees, and then mountains. Young Peter loves the mountains. He knows their names and often talks about them. When he is out driving along in his mom's van or his dad's truck he watches them. He says that they follow him, for wherever he goes he can see them in the distance. Young Peter is sure that the mountains can move. One day when he was out with his mom in her van he said, "Mountains moving, marching for a parade." His mom thought this was worth remembering and so she wrote it down on the calendar in the square that marked the day when they found out that Young Peter is a poet.

All children are poets. There is magic in their lives, for the experience of childhood takes place in a dimension different from that of our adult world. The mountains no longer move when we look at them, and sadly such possibilities are so far removed from our present-day apprehension of "reality" that we seldom give more than a smile to a small child's fancies. In our hurry to "educate" we think of childhood as a time of limited experience, and we talk of children "growing," "developing," and sometimes of "emerging." It is almost unthinkable for any of us to believe that the experiences of childhood may indeed be of a *higher order* than we, as adults, can even begin to comprehend. It is this proposition that will be explored in the present chapter.

The focus then is on childhood, and language is seen within that context. The visual representation that appears on page 96 is presented as one version of childhood. Two more will follow. The second is presented through a child's picture story and the third through a piece of prose. I believe that the same elements or structures are contained in each version of the "model," and that each serves to emphasize the limitations that we place on children when we refuse to recognize that the experience of childhood takes place in a dimension that is different from that of our adult world.

In the following discussion, much of the information that is gained from classroom observations and discussions with teachers can readily be understood, perhaps more so by you than by me. But I wonder about the insights to be gained from personal reflection on one's own childhood. As I prepared to write this piece, I found myself trying to explain the importance of such insights to myself before I could even begin to place them in the context of this chapter. That explanation is presented here as another layer of this piece about childhood and language that I would like to share.

In the 17th century the poet Henry Vaughan wrote:

> I cannot reach it; and my striving eye
> Dazzles at it, as at eternity.

Vaughan was writing about childhood—that alternative dimension from which we are all excluded. Childhood is beyond our imagination. It is another time and another place, lost to those who have "grown."

As adults, most of us know firsthand of the struggle necessary to reconcile the children that we were with the "grown-ups" that we have become. In connecting the halves of ourselves, the truth of imagination takes precedence over fact (see Coe, p. 84). All we have to hold in our heads are a few intimate details of some other part of ourselves, fleeting memories of children who no longer exist in a tangible way. We cannot produce these children for others to meet, nor can we ask them questions about ourselves.

Nowhere is our exclusion more evident than in the writings of those who would reconstruct their early lives. Eudora Welty puts it better than I could when she writes in her autobiography, *One writer's beginning*:

> My imagination takes its strength and guides its direction from what I see and hear and learn and feel and remember of my living world. But I was to learn slowly that both these worlds, outer and inner, were different from what they seemed to me in the beginning. (1983, p. 83)

But this does not stop her struggle to reach her other self. As a writer she can let the child, a new version of her old self, grow upon the page. Through words she makes the connection. Like Eudora Welty, I have learned that the only way I can come close to that alternative dimension is through the words that I write as I try to reconstruct my childhood. Admittedly, the few pieces that I have written are filtered through age and distorted by memory, but the child that I can produce in story is related to me. Language makes it possible for us to meet and get to know one another. We can play in the stories that I write. Through words, I too can make the connection.

Finding ourselves on paper may seem to be trivial, a little self-centered, and of no real importance for the children that we teach or the children that we love. Not so. Our perceptions of ourselves as children can help us to understand the experience of childhood in ways that no other experiment will allow.

Reading from Other Childhoods

But still, this is just the beginning. Our perceptions of ourselves as children need to be played against other childhoods, both real and imaginary. In *When the grass was taller: Autobiography and the experience of childhood*, Richard Coe presents more than 600 of these works. He defines the autobiography of childhood as a particular literary form, "a structure in which the succession of episodes presented by the text reflects more or less exactly the sequence of past experience" (p. 24). I have juxtaposed my writings on my own childhood with the autobiography and the experience of childhood as presented by Coe. I have added to these resources many of the ethnographic narratives of childhood experience that I have collected over the years. These collective writings, together with my classroom observations, and discussions with Suzanne Wiedenheft, a very special kindergarten teacher, have formed the comparative "data base" for the visual representation that appears on page 96.

In *Children's experience of place*, Hart (1979) speaks of engaging the landscape with the child. In many ways this visual representation is one attempt to achieve that aim. The emphasis is on childhood and the ways in which children communicate with objects and through objects as well as through words. It is a representation of children within their own environment, whether it be an apartment building on a busy city street or a farmhouse on a country dirt road, the (con)textual worlds of childhood begin wherever the young child lives. *A very small place* is

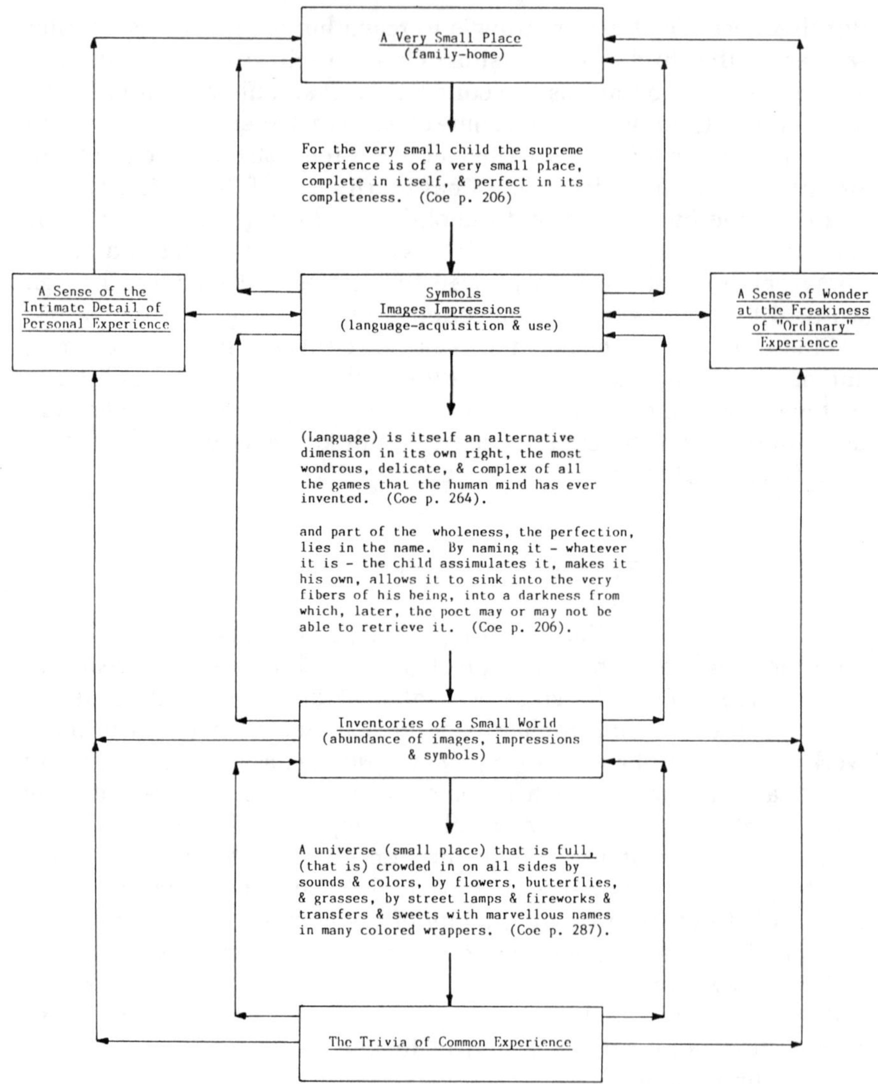

Figure 1.

home. It is a place filled with an abundance of objects, images and impressions, where nothing is trivial and details are not so much irrelevant as irrationally significant. In this place the child experiences a sense of wonder at the freakiness of "ordinary" events and an intense interest in the magic of plain and simple things. From these experiences, each child creates an authentic foundation for his or her own existence. Language is a part of that existence and is central to this interpretation of childhood.

Reflections of this view of childhood can be found in the lives of children, real and imaginary, past and present. *Inventories of a small world* can easily be recognized. In *Goodnight moon* by Margaret Wise Brown (1947), the notion is expressed through the comb and the brush and the bowl full of mush. In *Family literacy*, Laura Lindell presented as part of her own childhood inventory the outhouse and the potty chair from her early summers in Maine, Jessie Dawson gave a detailed description of the flowered wallpaper in her bedroom, and Lee Farley spoke of the swing that seemed to go "2-miles high." Trivial details remembered through the years. Writing of the autobiography of childhood, Richard Coe adds to these reflections when he states:

> Through this literature of childhood there runs a thin, glittering, transluscent vein of pure poetry, a kind of incantation, changing of the magical names of candies. From Royal Leamington Spa there come
>
> Chewy locust, thick strong liquorice sticks,
> Aniseed balls, bull's eye and sherbert. (Enright, *The terrible shears*, 1973, p. 33)

and from stricken and decidedly un-Royal South Shields:

> Dolly mixture, toffee-apples, "Mixed Shot," liquorice boot-laces, the wrapped lumps in the blue-and-white tins of Farrar's Original Harrogate Toffee . . . , Berwick Cockles, Edinburgh Rock, glacier mints and liquorice Allsorts, sherbert dabs, soda fountain. (Kirkup, *The only child*, 1957, p. 117)

Coe includes examples from Russia, Scotland, and Australia in his discussion of the importance of candies and the names of candies in the lives of the writers that he studied. In "real life," the reflections of objects that are irrationally significant can just as readily be found. For Young Peter, with whom this chapter began, those objects are the pieces of machinery that are used in the harvest of timber from the forests that surround his home. Peter talks of feller bunchers and cherry pickers, of skidders and chippers, of flat beds and hoists, and of log loaders and chain saws. He knows about wood chips and sawdust, boards and bark. He can tell you about the trees. He knows which is beech or oak or white pine, and he knows Mr. Bean, the chainsaw man.

Peter's interest in machinery and forestry gives us some inkling of the intimate detail of his personal experience. We can see him as an eyewitness of his everyday life, as he observes, learns, and talks about a world that we may never have seen or perhaps have forgotten. Peter's mother talks of learning from Peter about the world in which he lives. Many years ago Dororthy White wrote of similar learning experiences in *Books before five*:

> Now two and a half, Carol finds pictures everywhere, some of them pictures so small that they are overlooked by an adult eye until a child's pointing finger brings them into focus. Here is a soldier on a matchbox lid, there on the packet of razor blades is a man's head. To be in the house with her just now is a perpetual process of rediscovering one's own environment. Outside the house I notice this even more. As we walk up Garfield Avenue I share with her a new world around my own feet, the dandelions by the gutter, a piece of blue grass on the footpath, sparrows' droppings, locks on gates. (1983, p. 19)

What the child sees and what is important to the child is not self-evident. Peter's mother is learning as Carol's mother learned some 30 years ago that the small details of everyday life are important to young children. In Suzanne Wiedenheft's kindergarten classroom Emily teaches a similar lesson to Suzanne and the children when she brings her Pooh Bear in for show-and-tell. Pooh is made of yellow flannel and has a red waistcoat of a similar fabric. When it was Emily's turn for show and tell it was not Pooh that she shared but the tears in the fabric. She showed Suzanne and the children one of Pooh's paws and she said, "I have to be careful here so the stuffing doesn't come out." Suzanne asked her what kind of stuffing was inside Pooh. Emily said, "These little beads," and she took some out of the hole in Pooh's paw. One fell out on the floor but the children ignored it as they looked at the beads in Emily's hand. Then Emily showed the children and Suzanne some of the other holes in her Pooh Bear. "Did your mom sew them up?" Suzanne asked, noticing the stitching that had been used to close some of the holes. "No," Emily replied, "Hannah's mom did." Hannah smiled. Then Emily continued, "You see, Hannah's cat got Pooh. Here's another hole and here's one and here's another one." Hannah joined in the telling. She told Suzanne and the children that Emily had let her borrow Pooh Bear, and that her cat had played with it in the night while she was sleeping. In the morning the little beads had been all over the floor and with her mother's help she had picked them up and put them back inside the little bear.

Suzanne talked about Emily and Hannah and the importance of the tiny details of Pooh's experience. She also talked about their sense of wonder at his nighttime adventures. Emily and Hannah were able to share with Suzanne and the other children their intense interest in the magic of plain and simple things, and through Suzanne's retelling of the tale we can begin to appreciate the child's sense of wonder at the freakiness of "ordinary" experience. Russell Baker adds to this appreciation when he writes in his autobiography:

> On those occasions when my father took me to Brunswick, the supreme delight was to have Uncle Lewis seat me on a board placed across the

> arms of his barber chair, crank me into the sky, and subject me to the pampered luxury of being clippered, snipped, and doused with heavy applications of Lucky Tiger or Jeris hair tonic, which left my hair plastered gorgeously to the sides of my head and sent me into the street reeking of aromatic delight. (1982, p. 52)

The authenticity of Russell Baker's memories of the magic of the personal details of everyday life can be verified in the lives of today's young children. One Saturday morning a few weeks ago, Ellen (who is 7) did not come downstairs for the longest time. Ellen usually gets up early on Saturdays, and enjoys making her own breakfast. Anne, Ellen's mom, knew that Ellen was awake and wondered what she was doing. Eventually she went to visit Ellen in her room. Ellen was sitting up in bed and she was finishing a story. This is what she had written (Figure 2 and 2a),

> When I liy in bed, beefor I go to
> sleep at nitghe I see a
> streek of lhite shooting
> cross the holl.
> And *when* I wake
> I see a streek of
> shatoe, shooting cross
> the holl. I can
>
> side two
>
> never see the frunt I
> can owase see the
> back.
> By Ellen Perkins.
> Titel. When I liy in
> bed.

Ellen explained to Anne that she often watched the streak of light before she went to sleep but that she had never known what caused it to shine across the hall. Then she showed her mother the picture (Figure 3) she had drawn of herself lying in bed looking at the lamp in the hall. She told her mother that she had gotten out of bed to see where the light and the shadow came from and she found that it was from the lamp hanging outside of her bedroom. Then she said that although she couldn't see the lamp from her bed she decided to put it in her picture. Anne smiled when she told the story, and said she had not known about this part of Ellen; she spoke of thinking about Ellen's going to sleep at night watching the light that shone into her room. It was an image of her child that she had not considered before.

In presenting the visual representation of the (con)textual worlds of childhood it is important to emphasize that an openness of meaning is

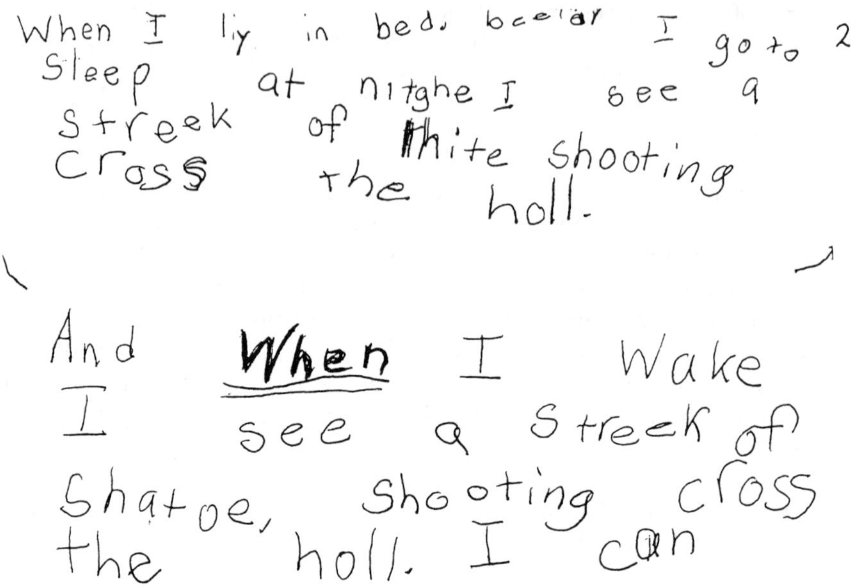

When I liy in bed. bcelar I go to 2
Sleep at nitghe I see a
streek of white shooting
cross the holl.

And When I wake
I see a streek of
Shatoe, shooting cross
the holl. I can

Figure 2.

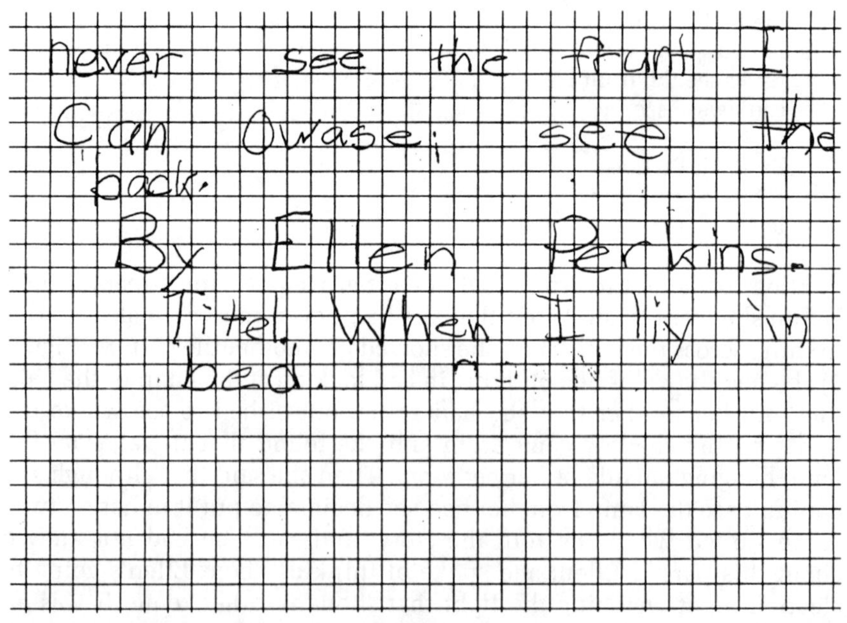

never see the frunt I
Can owase; see the
back.
By Ellen Perkins.
Titel When I liy in
bed.

Figure 2a.

Figure 3.

essential. I have deliberately tried to slip from one interpretation to another without separating the "categories," for I believe that through multiple interpretations all of the categories can be illustrated in a single childhood experience. The model is helpful for the purposes of coherence in theoretical description, but the visual representation could just as easily be a picture from a story by a child or an autobiographical piece on the experience of childhood written in later years. Both these representations follow.

The second version of the visual representation comes from a page of a book that Ellen made when she was just 6. On the first page of the book (Figure 4) Ellen introduces herself: "I AM ELLEN"; her dog, "I AM LILY"; and one of her cats, "I AM OLLIE." In the picture Ollie is thinking about Ellen pouring him a bowl of milk.

In the second picture (Figure 5), the one that we will be discussing, Ollie is asleep, "zzzzzzzz" and dreaming again of Ellen pouring milk and also of her Dad building a cat house. The picture is of a very small place. Ollie is sleeping on a table in Ellen's house. The picture is filled with an abundance of objects, images, and symbols. Ellen's lunch box is on the table beside Ollie. Dad is holding a saw and an ax, and he is sawing a piece of wood which is placed on top of the house that he is making for the cat. In Ellen's hand is a jug of milk and she is pouring milk into a bowl. Ollie is thinking and Ellen is interpreting (reading)

Figure 4

Figure 5

Figures 4 and 5. Ellen's cat pictures first appeared in *Family storybook reading*, Heinemann Educational Books, 1986 (Denny Taylor & Dorothy S. Strickland).

his dreams, and she is writing them down for her mom and dad to read. The picture is of trivial everyday events; Ellen often pours milk for her cats and her dad is always making something. Through the picture we can begin to gain some understanding of Ellen's sensitivity to the intimate detail of her own personal experience, and her sense of wonder at the freakiness of "ordinary" experience. Ellen can imagine her cat Ollie dreaming while he sleeps and she can interpret his dreams. Language is indeed the most wondrous, delicate, and complex of all the games that we can play.

The third version of the visual representation is an autobiographical story that was written several years ago. In the story of *Rosie Llewellyn and her grandad's bath*, similar structures to those in Ellen's story are made visible and we can get another look at the alternative dimensions of childhood experience.

"Rosie," Grandad shouted a whisper up the stairs. "Have our Sarah while I have a bath. She can come back down when I've finished."

"Come on Sarah," I called quietly, as I sat up in bed and leaned back against the pillows. "Come and cwch with me."

Sarah started up the stairs and as she passed the twist at the bottom I heard our Grandad shut the door. It was quiet for a moment; Sarah had stopped climbing. I could almost feel her holding her breath in temper. I held my breath and waited. Then, with a rush of air she was climbing again, hitting each step with her angry feet. She was making enough noise to wake old Florrie Lewis, who lived next door, let alone our Nan and brother Tommy who were asleep in the front bedroom.

"Be quiet Sarah," I shouted in a whisper as loud as our Grandad's, "you'll wake up Nan and our Tommy."

Sarah appeared in the doorway, a furious little thing with a stubborn chin and scowling eyes.

"Come on, there's a good girl," I said, "we can have a cuddle until Grandad's had a bath. Then we'll go down and have a cup of tea with him."

Sarah looked at me hard. "Why can't I stay down with him?"

"You're getting too big," I said, and then to make her feel better I added, "I had to stay upstairs when I got to be a big girl like you."

"Why?"

"Because I stared at him when he took his trousers off I suppose."

Sarah looked down. "He looks so funny," she said.

"Not really," I smiled, "it would be awful if we all looked the same now wouldn't it."

Sarah raised her eyes and smiled. She took a run at the pile of lumpy old mattresses and grabbed for the blankets to help her up. She crawled, hands and knees, to the top of the bed and got under the covers beside me. Then we slid under the blankets and giggled wicked thoughts in delicious contentment.

While Sarah hid beneath the bedclothes I thought of the time when I was a little girl and I watched my Grandad wash himself in an old zinc bath. Each morning I'd lie in bed and wait for him to come home, and when I heard him moving about in the kitchen I'd make my way down the dark narrow stairs, watch out for the twist at the bottom, and feel for the latch to open the door. As the door swung open I'd see my Grandad sitting in his chair having a whiff, smoking tobacco and drinking tea. He was a tiny man who seemed enormous to me. Covered in coal dust and steaming from working in water, he seemed magical and strange. He would look up and nod at me as I stepped down into the room, and then he'd point with his chin and his pipe to the chair on the opposite side of the fire.

I'd cross the room and climb onto the chair and there I'd sit drinking the tea that he tipped into his saucer and watching him as he got ready for his bath. He'd pour water from the giant iron kettles that were bubbling on the fire into the old zinc bath that he'd carried in from the backyard. Then he'd take off his old jacket, his Welsh flannel shirt and woolen singlet, before he sat back on his chair, to untie his boots and undo the leather yorks that kept his trousers out of the water and close to his body. Once the yorks were untied, he'd kneel down on the floor beside the bath, and begin to wash the coal dust from his body. He'd take a half-pound of white kitchen soap, rub it on a flannel and then rub the flannel on his head. Little black streams formed in the wrinkles on his face and trickled down onto his neck, and as they went, I could see underneath the familiar pinkness of my Grandad's head. The muck and grime was washed away and he'd polish his bald spot on the towel that was warming on the brass rod of the mantlepiece. He washed his top half and scrubbed it so clean that it seemed disconnected from his lower half which was still encased in his steaming trousers. The smell of the damp clothing drying on his body filled the room with the workings of the mine, and of the stall, the place where my Grandad worked on his knees with a manvil and shovel to cut the coal from the narrow seams of the Kay's Slope coalface.

Once his top half was clean he'd stand up, turn his back to me and unbutton his trousers, drop them to his knees and then sit down on his chair to pull them off his legs. Stiff and crusty, it was useless to wash them, they were too filthy for that. He just put them on a kitchen chair with the legs dangling over the back so that they would continue to dry and be ready for the next night. Again he turned his back, this time to unbutton his long johns and pull them off. The blueness of his coal-dust body left him not quite naked and as he turned he held his hand over the place that he didn't want me to see. He stepped into the bath and lowered himself carefully into the water so that none of it would slop over the top onto the floor.

He sat facing the other way and sometimes I would soap his back making patterns in the navy blue bubbles. His skin was stretched tight and did not give under my fingers. It wasn't soft and fleshy like our Nan's; it was firm and springy and pulled white over the bumps of his spine. When his back was as clean as his front and his feet were soaped and rinsed, Grandad would stand to wash between his legs. Then I would look at the things that dangled from his body. They were wrinkled and soft and much darker than the blue white skin of his back or the pinkness of his head, and when he washed them with the soapy cloth they moved around and then swung free as he bent down to rinse the cloth in the murky water of the old zinc bath. Each day as I watched my fascination grew, and I would stare at him as he washed them, wondering if working down the mines had made these strange things grow. Finally my Grandad told me to turn my back when he stood up in the bath, but my curiosity got the better of me and I would stand with my back to him bending forward to look through my legs. To my surprise our Grandad knew I was still looking and he must have told Nan because she told me I couldn't go downstairs when he first got home. I was to wait until he'd had his bath. She said he'd call me when he'd finished.

"Rosie," he would whisper up the stairs and I would climb out of bed and hurry down. There he'd be, sitting in his chair, pink and clean in his Welsh flannel shirt, smoking his pipe and drinking tea. He'd nod as I stepped into the room and put his tea down so that he could help me onto his lap. Then he'd pour some of the darkly brewed mixture into a saucer and together we'd sit sipping our tea, enjoying the quiet before the morning began.

The bedclothes were growing hot and stuffy and I forgot our Grandad and his old zinc bath as I tried to escape from the tangle of sheets.

"Do you think we can go down now?" Sarah asked as she wriggled her way to the top of the bed.

"Grandad will call us when he's ready," I said pushing back the bedclothes before we suffocated. Downstairs I could hear our Grandad raking the coals in the fire, making it hot for our Nan to cook breakfast when she went down. Then the door at the bottom of the stairs opened and Grandad called up.

"Sarah, come and have some tea," and to me he added, "and you Rosie."

Rosie Llewellyn's story takes place in her Nan and Grandad's coal miner's cottage. The story is filled with an abundance of objects, images and symbols from that small world. In it she writes of the narrow stairs closed off by the downstairs door, the beds high with lumpy mattresses, the tea that she drank from her Grandad's saucer, and of course, her Grandad, who was so magical and strange. Through the story, the interconnections are made and again we are given the opportunity to peep through the cracks and to see for one moment the alternative dimensions of childhood experience that we have learned (been taught?) to ignore and have since forgotten.

Postscript

Yesterday the postman brought me yet another envelope stuffed with ideas for teachers of reading. This one began with the question, "Where in the world can you find *all the word lists you may ever need* . . . all ready for instant use?" I suppose the assumption is that the words that we come up with when we pull language apart are the words that are needed by the young child. One wonders if Young Peter's feller buncher is on one of those lists, or if the publishers are aware that it is the holes in Pooh Bear that are important to Emily. Do they know that it is the light and shadow from the lamp outside Ellen's room that captures her imagination and inspires her story? We have come so far from the child's world. We have replaced our recognition of the authenticity of their experiences of childhood with a prepackaged world that does not recognize that the child's experiences may be of a higher order than we as adults can even begin to understand. The limitations that we impose are unnecessary. Classrooms are a part of the child's small world and we can fill them with an abundance of objects, images and symbols that are meaningful to the young child. There is room for children to create their own magic when researchers and teachers recognize the authenticity of their experience, and see learning as a joint enterprise between adults and children, rather than imposing a system that encourages and often demands a one-way transfer of knowledge. We can begin ourselves by considering *imaginatively* what the smallness of our prepackaged world is likely to mean to the young children that we parent, study and teach.

References

Baker, R. (1982). *Growing up*. New York: Congdon & Weed.

Brown, M. W. (1947). *Goodnight moon*. New York: Harper & Row.

Coe, R. N. (1984). *When the grass was taller: Autobiography and the experience of childhood*. New Haven, CN: Yale University Press.

Enright, D. J. (1973). *The terrible shears.* (quoted by Coe in *When the grass was taller: Autobiography and the experience of childhood.*)

Hart, R. (1979). *Children's experience of place.* New York: Irvington.

Kirkup, J. (1957) *The only child.* (Quoted by Coe in *When the grass was taller: Autobiography and the experience of childhood.*)

Taylor, D. *Rosie Llewelyn and her grandad's bath.* Collection of unpublished stories.

Welty, E. (1983). *One writer's beginnings.* Warner Books Edition, 1984. (Original publication by Harvard University Press.)

White, D. (1983). *Books before five.* Portsmouth, NH: Heinemann Educational Books. (original publication by NZCER, 1954.)

PART II

THE LANGUAGE MILIEU

Chapter 7

Language and the Transmission of Values: Implications from Japanese Day Care

Irene S. Shigaki

New York University

Transmission of values to the young is crucial to the survival and maintenance of a culture. While the process varies from culture to culture, language plays a central role in inculcating values in all modern societies. Bloomfield (1945), a linguist, explains:

> Every language serves as the bearer of a culture. If you speak a language you take part, to some degree, in the way of living represented by that language. Each system of culture has its own way of looking at things and people and of dealing with them. To the extent that you have learned to speak and understand a foreign tongue, to that extent you have learned to respond with a different selection and emphasis to the world around you, and for your relations with people you have gained a new system of sensibilities, considerations, conventions, and restraints. (p. 625)

Yet, although language is inextricably linked to culture and the transmission of values of that culture, it is only one of several modalities used in the process of instilling values in the young.

Nonverbal means are also important in the inculcation of values. In fact, verbal and nonverbal modes usually interact, with the verbal message reinforcing the nonverbal and vice versa. Some societies, such as the Japanese, seem to have more highly developed means of nonverbal communication than we do (e.g., Reischauer, 1977; Suzuki, 1978). Reischauer even suggests that the Japanese "have a positive mistrust of verbal skills, thinking that these tend to show superficiality in contrast to inner, less articulate feelings that are communicated by innuendo or by nonverbal means" (p. 136). A Japanese sociolinguist, Honna (1975), qualifies this statement with his claim that "the consciousness of the role of language as an indispensable means of harmonious human relations belongs to the new postwar value system" (p. 208). One can thus conclude that even in Japanese society, where nonverbal forms of communication have been highly developed, language still serves to reinforce values independently and in interaction with nonverbal cues.

When examining the role of language in the transmission of values in a foreign culture, it is essential that one recognize the problems inherent in the examination of translated language. Nuances of meaning are often distorted in making translations, even between languages belonging to the same family of languages such as the Indo-European group. This problem is severely compounded when attempting to translate across family groups as is the case with English and Japanese (Whorf, 1956). A crucial problem is that words do not have exact equivalents in both languages (Passin, 1982; Suzuki, 1978). Suzuki, a Japanese scholar who has written extensively in the area of sociolinguistics, points out that "each language slices the world differently, each at different angles and in different ways" (p. 23). A helpful illustration which he provides is the discrepancy in meaning from one language to another of the word "nose." In English it denotes the olfactory organ. The Japanese *hana* embraces this meaning but also includes the trunk of an elephant, while in Turkish *burun* includes the English definition, but also the beak of a bird (pp. 62–63). Thus, while accuracy in the translation of key phrases in the sections below is the goal, it must be acknowledged that inherent in the translation process may be a margin of ambiguity and imprecision.

The focus of this chapter is the contribution of language in the transmission of values to young children in Japanese group care. The thesis is that even during infancy and toddlerhood, when language skills are still in a formative phase, language serves as an effective vehicle for reinforcing nonverbal messages and contributing to the inculcation of societal values.

Data reported below come from firsthand observations of several dozen Japanese day-care centers (full day care for children from 4 months to age 6) and kindergartens (half-day programs for children from ages 3 to 6). The primary focus is on children from 6 months to age 3, though relevant illustrations drawn from observations of older children are also cited.[1]

[1] The bulk of the data reported was gathered during two sabbaticals spent in Japan—the 1978–79 academic year and the spring term in 1983, supplemented by several briefer trips. An earlier article (Shigaki, 1983) describes in detail the settings and conditions

Key Japanese Values

Japanese caregivers, queried as to the kind of child they try to foster, identified attributes which can be divided into two clusters of values (Shigaki, 1983). The first cluster includes qualities conducive to harmonious human relationships. Terms frequently used to describe goals were sympathetic-empathetic (*omoiyari*), gentle (*yasashii*), socially conscious (*shakaisei*), kind (*shinsetsu*), and cooperative-harmonious (*kyochosei*). The second cluster comprises two interrelated concepts: patience or perseverance (*nintai*), and concentration (*shuchuryoku*). The significance of these clusters of values as reflectors of general values of Japanese society has already been well documented (e.g., Caudill, 1973; Clark, 1978; Lebra, 1976). The social anthropologists White and LeVine (1986) have cautioned, however, that the two clusters are intertwined. They acknowledge the importance of perseverance and concentration, but feel these qualities are only visible manifestations of deeper abilities to be a good, social person (p. 56). Support for this view can be found in some of the vignettes reported under Cluster II below.

Cluster I: Harmonious Human Relationships

MacEachron (1983) notes that one aspect of early Japanese education deserving of special attention is that, "In the early years of formal education, great emphasis is placed upon socializing the children, teaching them to work and play together harmoniously" (p. 3). It is the contention of this paper that socialization is evident even *earlier* for those children in day care and preschools in Japan. Not only is the preschool a socializing agency, but it serves as an important reference group as well. Lebra (1976) explains that school-age children derive their identity primarily from the school they attend (p. 23). Understandably, other aspects of harmonious human relationships are first cultivated in the home. From in-depth interviews with 57 Japanese women, Lebra (1984) found that mothers encouraged their children to be *yasashii* (tender) and to have *omoiyari* (empathetic kindness) toward others (p. 186).

---

under which observations were made during 1978–79. Several dozen public and private day care centers and kindergartens were visited in both urban and rural settings. Five of these facilities were visited periodically over several years with extended observations made in both the roles of participant–observer and researcher. The latter role included formal timed observations of 50 children from 6 to 36 months in age during which a record was made of both activities and language. Several of the vignettes presented in this chapter were originally reported in Shigaki (1983).

How is the value of harmonious human relationships transmitted to children in group care? Tangible nonverbal forms of group identity, such as school uniforms, are commonly seen in Japanese day-care and kindergarten settings. Classes composed strictly of age peers often wear color-coded name tages designating school and class membership. Lebra (1984) also noted group synchronization of action (p. 194), and observations in preschools support this. By the age of 2, a regular part of the daily schedule is group rhythmic movement to recorded music. From this age, children are heard responding in unison to greetings. In rural Japan where the playgrounds are more spacious, more than 100 4- and 5-year-olds can be observed performing their daily exercises in unison.

A usual practice in Japanese preschools is also the use of specific names to identify each class. Names of flowers or of animals appear to be popular. For example, the 1's class might be called *sakura-gumi*—cherry group, while the 2's may be called *churippu-gumi*—tulip group, or alternatively one class might be referred to as *risu-gumi*—squirrel group, while the other might be *kirin-gumi*—giraffe group. Teachers verbally reinforce the sense of group identity by regularly addressing the class by its name.

With older children, ages 4 and 5, small groups within the class often function as units for such activities as meals and chores. Special names are used to designate these smaller groups as well. Membership in these groups usually reflects a wide cross-section of abilities (Lewis, 1984). It is interesting to note that in American early childhood classrooms, group names usually denote ability subgroups in the class. As a result, the names can connote, for example, membership in either the best reading group or the poorest reading group. These subgroup names can create a competitive or divisive tone in the classroom. Group names used in Japanese preschools, on the other hand, function to strengthen membership bonds.

Despite the formulation of class membership based on strict grouping by age, there are ample opportunities in Japanese preschool settings for cross-age interactions. During free play, which is usually an extension of the morning arrival period, children are often free to visit other classes. During the day, an entire class may visit a neighboring class. These cross-age interactions help foster in the child a sense of where he or she belongs in the age hierarchy. Perhaps this is a precursor of the importance of vertical relationships found in Japanese social groupings, as described by Nakane (1972).

Unlike English, Japanese has specific words denoting older and younger brothers, and older and younger sisters. There are even specific words to denote first-born son or daughter, second-born son or daughter, and so forth. In fact, it used to be common practice to give sons names that denoted their birth order: Ichiro or Taro (first-born son), Jiro (second-born son), and so forth. During cross-age interactions, one might hear a caregiver refer to the older child in a dyad as *onisan* (older brother). Suzuki explains this practice in the following manner:

> Kinship terms used by an older family member in a dialogue with a younger member are in the final analysis based on the adoption of the youngest member's perspective. Both the person addressed and the person referred to are represented by the terms that show their positions in the family as seen by the youngest member. (pp. 123–124)

In a Japanese family setting, children do not refer to their elder siblings by name, but as *onisan*—older brother, or *onesan*—older sister. Conversely, older siblings do refer to younger siblings by name, often attaching the diminutive *chan*. These practices have also carried over to group-care settings. They serve to reinforce the responsibility of an older child for a younger one and help engender respect in a younger child for his elders.

Suzuki further illustrates his point regarding the adoption of the younger member's perspective by citing the common practice of calling the only or youngest son using the masculine first-person pronoun *boku*—I. By doing so, parents refer to the child from the perspective of the youngest member in the family, in this case the child himself (p. 124). This is also customary in classes of young children. Young girls referring to themselves as *boku*, on the other hand, are corrected with the explanation that *boku* is used only by boys.

Japanese parents call each other and refer to themselves as "papa" or "*otoosan*" and "mama" or "*okaasan*" as the case may be, rather than calling each other by their first names. This practice was deemed noteworthy by a school psychologist providing background information on the children of Japanese nationals attending American schools (Karan, 1984). An extreme example of this practice was exhibited by Japanese acquaintances who had been married for some time, but were unable to have children, but nevertheless called each other "*otoosan*" or "*okaa san*."

Unrelated adults might also be called "*obasan*"—auntie or "*ojisan*"—uncle. One young caregiver was heard objecting to being called *obasan* by one of the children in her charge, feeling that *onesan* (older sister) was more appropriate given her age.

In short, the various forms of address and self-reference reinforce respective roles within the social hierarchy. Suzuki explains:

> Japanese terms of self-reference and address may be construed as serving to specify and confirm the concrete roles for the speaker and the addressee.

> "Role" may be defined here as a concept referring to a specific pattern of behavior which an individual with specific qualifications and qualities generally demonstrates within a given social context. (p. 129)

The emphasis on role is further strengthened by the relatively infrequent use of personal pronouns in Japanese (Pei, 1949, p. 380). This de-emphasis on the self, combined with the use of role-related terms of self-reference and address, contributes to a group sense.

Japanese caregivers also directly enjoin their charges to play harmoniously together. A common word used in these contexts is *naka-yoku*, defined as "on good friendly terms," or "in peace, harmony, concord with" (Masuda, 1974, p. 1177). Two vignettes illustrate the use of this term:

1. A toddler almost 2 is the biggest and one of the oldest in his group. Several cardboard boxes are set out for the children to play with. First, Hiroshi stands on one box. Then he tries to usurp the box of another child, making the child cry. The caregiver admonishes him. The toddler then joins two children standing on a box and soon tries to push them off. The caregiver carries him off the box. Hiroshi gets into another box. A child tries to get into the box with him, at which point the caregiver encourages them to: "*Naka-yoku asobi masho*"—"Let's play nicely together."

2. A group of four toddlers and their caregiver are crowded around an aquarium containing several large snails. In the process of jockeying for a better position, Naomi hits the child next to her. The caregiver admonishes: "*Naka-yoku asobi masho.*"

Already by the preschool years some Japanese children have learned to sanction cooperative behavior positively. As is the practice in much of Asia, most teachers in private preschools have the responsibility not only for the care of their children, but also for cleaning their classrooms. After spending the day with a 3's class, I began assisting the teacher by sweeping the floor while the children were quietly engaged in independent seatwork. Seeing this, one child remarked: "*Sensei to Irene-san wa naka-yoku osooji o shite imasu*"—"Teacher and Miss Irene are cleaning harmoniously together."

Cluster II: Perseverance and Concentration

In a prize-winning essay, Morsbach (1978) notes:

> When someone is undergoing training in Japan, it is a commonly held belief that the body is greatly malleable as long as the will is strong enough. The terms "*gaman suru*" (to persevere) and "*ganbare!*" (hold

out!) are often heard in this context, and have a very positive flavour. (p. 7)

Consistent with Morsbach's contention, Japanese day-care workers are often heard using these very words as they encourage their charges to persevere. Illustrative of this point are the following vignettes providing a sampling of such situations:

1. Aya-chan, age 13 months, was physically the smallest in her group. The other larger children frequently grabbed what she was playing with, usually eliciting a loud cry of protest from Aya-chan. Rather than reprimanding the larger children, the caregivers generally responded: "Aya-chan, *ganbare*"—"Aya-chan don't give up." (When the caregivers were asked why the other children tended to pick on Aya-chan, they said they felt that it was because she usually reacted to their overtures by crying loudly. Hence, they were encouraging her to react to the ill treatment from others more stoically. Lewis [1984] reports observing a similar situation in a Japanese nursery school.)

2. A group of eight toddlers from 14 to 20 months was headed from their second-floor room to the outdoor playground. As they reached the stairs, the caregivers reminded them to hang on to the railing, which was fixed at an appropriate height for their use. The toddlers slowly descended the staircase a step at a time in single file. As the children reached the bottom of the stairs, they sat on the landing together with one of the caregivers, clapping rhythmically and chanting encouragingly to those still descending the stairs: "Ma-chan, *ganbare*!" "At-chan, *ganbare*!" "Akiko-chan, *ganbare*!"

3. Three 2-year-olds were sitting snugly together in a large cardboard box. When a fourth child squeezed his way into the box as well, one of the children already in the box began to cry. A caregiver nearby encouraged the crying child with: "*Gaman, gaman*"—"Bear with it."

4. A group of children was practicing for an athletic event by running across a large college field. The youngest, 2½, fell when he was halfway across the field and burst into tears. The caregivers at the finish line yelled encouragingly: "*Ganbare*!" Still crying, the child picked himself up and finished the course, then he was warmly embraced and praised for his perseverance.

5. In a relay, 4-year-olds were competing in the usual two groups. The team that was behind received much encouragement from the spectators: "*Ganbare*!"—"Keep on trying, don't give up!"

No convenient one-word equivalents in English come readily to mind for the Japanese word *ganbare* and *gaman*. It may be that these values are not given the same weight in America as in Japan. In fact, interesting implications can be drawn regarding the contrasting value structures held by American and Japanese caregivers to the above. In all the vignettes, the emphasis is on encouraging children to cope sturdily with adversity and/or to complete the task that they have begun. American caregivers, on the other hand, would more likely chastise children for picking on someone smaller as in the first vignette, and encourage the interloper to wait his or her turn rather than squeeze into an already full box as described in the third vignette. In contrast, in the latter case, the Japanese emphasis is also on including the latecomer in the group despite the discomfort that may result. Again, as illustrated by the fourth vignette, the Japanese would value the overcoming of adversity and perseverance, while the American caregiver probably would rush out onto the field to provide the child with immediate comfort, relegating the value of persistence to a secondary position.

Persistence entails both a long attention span and concentration in the short run and willingness to engage in the self-discipline required to devote years of training which may lead to eventual mastery in the long run. Westerners, on the other hand, often look for shortcuts or expect to become instant experts (Morsbach, 1978). From her observations of both Japanese and American kindergartens, the anthropologist Lanham (1966) concluded that: "An uninterrupted attention span of long duration was characteristic of the Japanese but not of the American children" (p. 331). Evidence of extended attention spans was observed in many of the Japanese day-care settings as well.

The examples below illustrate the role of language in sustaining attention. It should be pointed out, however, that the length of children's attention spans was influenced by other factors, such as the nature of the task. Certain interactions with caregivers also promoted longer attention spans. These included story reading, structured movement to records, and opportunities for extended labeling, such as naming all the colors of the crayons in a box.

1. With toddlers from 12 to 18 months, the average observed time on task for all activities was a little over 4 minutes. Hiro-chan, a boy 14 months of age, sustained the longest play bout of any child in this age range, playing continuously with blocks for almost 14½ minutes. The child had initially been withdrawn, having just returned to day care after an absence of about a month. When he began to finger some small blocks, the caregiver skillfully began to interact with him exclaiming: "What do you suppose it is?" Gradually she began to stack the blocks, allowing the child to knock them down. She talked to Hiro-chan in the process. "Let's do it one more time." "Wait until it's tall." "This time let's do it over here," she said as she pushed the blocks closer to the child. "This time you do the stacking." Soon she had Hiro-chan stacking the blocks himself, knocking them down, then starting over. At one point she had to leave for a few minutes, but the child

was able to sustain the activity on his own. Upon her return, he was encouraged to explore the stacking properties of different shaped blocks, triangular blocks as compared with rectangular blocks, and so forth.

2. Three children who had recently turned 2 sat in a large cardboard box together with a caregiver. First, they bathed themselves, accompanied by a counting song sung by the caregiver. When one of the children began to shake the box, the caregiver cried: "An earthquake, oh, oh!" After calm had returned, she began to 'shampoo' the head of each child. "Don't get soap in your ears." "Rinse." "Are you clean?" "Splendid!" Almost 15 minutes had elapsed by the time the children were ready to leave their "tub."

3. By ages 2½ to 3, the average length of play bouts was observed to be a little over 6 minutes. However, in this age span there was considerable variability. The longest play bout lasted 36½ minutes, when a child was involved in a crayon resist project. Language proficiency had become sufficiently functional by this age that children were able to sustain imaginative play with their peers without the presence of an adult. A 35-month-old girl and a 36-month-old boy had been good friends since they entered day care at the same time the year before. They were observed playing together with housekeeping materials, pretending that they were in a restaurant. Megumi would make something, serve it to Hayato, and elicit his reactions. They played together in this fashion, chatting freely for 12 minutes at which time Hayato wandered out of the area. After a few minutes Megumi called him back by telling him he had a telephone call! The two resumed play for another 5 minutes, this time lying down together, organizing a pile of pillows around them.

4. The most unusual extended play bout observed was that of 30-month-old Chi-chan, who carried a live rooster about on the playground for 20 minutes. The caregiver praised her for her skill at holding the rooster, and encouraged her to allow other children to hold it as well. Only one other child was willing to and then only briefly. A small group clustered around Chi-chan, discussing the rooster's eyes and how sleepy he looked. In the middle of the discussion, Chi-chan wandered away, still carrying the rooster, encouraging it to sleep, and singing to it as she walked about.

The observed length of play bouts reported above compare favorably with those reported by Sylva, Roy, and Painter (1980) in a study of older children from 3½ to 5½ years old in Britain. Mean length of play bout for activities where excellent concentration was observed were reported to be: 6.3 minutes for art, 5.1 minutes for small-scale construction, and 5.0 minutes for pretending. Some play bouts of 10 minutes or more were also mentioned. The mean length of bouts for differing activities, however, ranged from 1.3 to 6.3 minutes (pp. 67–68).

Conclusions

The thesis of this chapter is that language is an important vehicle for the transmission of values even in infancy and toddlerhood, when the child's language competence is still in a formative stage. Admittedly, the role of language in reinforcing nonverbal cues and contributing to the inculcation of values can be more readily discerned within the context of Japanese society, where there is generally a consensus between the home and school as to which values should be nurtured.

In contrast, America can be characterized as a pluralistic society in which competing and sometimes conflicting value structures coexist. Perhaps in part due to this diversity, we depend upon language more than the Japanese do to communicate our feelings, needs, and desires. Given the primacy of language for communication in American society, it has greater potential for influencing values transmission than in Japan. Caregivers need to examine their verbal messages to ensure that they are sanctioning desirable values. Congruence between verbal and nonverbal messages is essential to avoid conflicting messages. Given the pluralistic nature of our society, we need to communicate a sense of respect for different value structures so that children are not placed in the untenable position of conflicting loyalties such as between two caregivers or between the home and the school.

References

Bloomfield, L. (1945). About foreign language teaching. *The Yale Review*, *34*, 625–641.

Caudill, W. A. (1973). The influence of social structure and culture on human behavior in modern Japan. *Journal of Nervous and Mental Disease*, *157*, 240–257.

Clark, G. (1978). The human-relations society and the ideological society. *Japan Foundation Newsletter*, 6(3), 2–7.

Honna, N. (1975). A note on social structure and linguistic behavior: A case study of Japanese community. In F. C. C. Peng (Ed.), *Language in Japanese society: Current issues in sociolinguistics* (pp. 193–214). University of Tokyo Press.

Karan, V. (1984, April). *Dealing with Japanese students*. Unpublished manuscript, Fort Lee, NJ.

Lanham, B. B. (1966). The psychological orientation of the mother–child relationship in Japan. *Monumenta Nipponica*, *21*, 322–333.

Lebra, T. S. (1976). *Japanese patterns of behavior*. Honolulu: University Press of Hawaii.

Lebra, T. S. (1984). *Japanese women: Constraint and fulfillment*. Honolulu: University of Hawaii Press.

Lewis, C. C. (1984). Cooperation and control in Japanese nursery schools. *Comparative Education Review, 28*(1), 69–84.

MacEachron, D. (1983). What can America learn from Japan. *IHJ Bulletin* (Tokyo: The International House of Japan), *3*(3), 1–7.

Masuda, K. (Ed.). (1974). *Kenkyusha's new Japanese–English dictionary* (4th ed.). Tokyo: Kenkyusha.

Morsbach, H. (1978, December 20). Socio-psychological aspects of persistence in Japan. *Japan Times*, p. 7.

Nakane, C. (1972). *Japanese society*. Los Angeles: University of California Press.

Passin, H. (1982). *Encounter with Japan*. New York: Kodansha.

Pei, M. (1949). *The story of language*. New York: Lippincott.

Reischauer, E. O. (1977). *The Japanese*. Cambridge, MA: Belknap Press.

Shigaki, I. S. (1983). Child care practices in Japan and the United States: How do they reflect cultural values in young children? *Young Children, 38*(4), 13–24.

Suzuki, T. (1978). *Japanese and the Japanese: Words in culture* (A. Mirua, Trans.). New York: Kodansha (Original work published 1973).

Sylva, K., Roy, C., & Painter, M. (1980). *Childwatching at playgroup and nursery school*. Ypsilanti, MI: High/Scope Press.

White, M. I., & LeVine, R. A. (1986). What is an *ii ko* (good child)? In H. Stevenson, H. Azuma, & K. Hakuta (Eds.), *Child development and education in Japan*. New York: W. H. Freeman.

Whorf, B. L. (1956). *Language, thought, and reality* (J. B. Carroll, Ed.). Cambridge, MA: MIT Press.

Chapter 8

Bilingualism, Early Language, and Cognitive Development

Angela Carrasquillo

Fordham University

The early childhood years have long been recognized as the most important period in the educational and emotional development of a human being. Language development and language foundation are required components for the child's growth and academic development. Language is a means to unlock the student's mental powers. Language provides individuals with the innate capability to understand and form grammatical sentences and to produce utterances at a given time. It is a creative process used to understand what others say, to communicate their own ideas and to get meaning and satisfaction from the language environment. Language in the classroom is both a process and a product, and it can enter the curriculum in two ways: as a system of communication and as a meaning of learning.

Much debate has been going on the issue of using two languages for communication and instructional purposes. There are different points of view, especially when the relationship is made between bilingualism, early bilingualism and cognitive development. This article intends to summarize recent points of views toward the relationship of these three variables.

Bilingualism: A Definition

For purposes of this article bilingualism is the regular use of two or more languages. Bilingualism gives individuals the opportunity to become fully articulate, literate and educated in two languages and sensitive to two or more cultures. Bilingualism provides students with a functional language competence and understanding of the history and culture influencing the values, beliefs and attitudes of different cultural groups. There is the need to produce competent bilinguals, able to cope with a highly interdependent and multilingual world. Bilingualism is present in practically every country of the world (Belgium, Canada, Czechoslovakia, Finland, Israel, Philippines, South Africa, Switzerland, and Wales) in all classes of society and in all age groups. Bilingualism is a phenomenon that has existed since the beginning of language in human history.

Presently, the most popular type of bilingualism in the United States is transitional bilingualism. It has been the predominant mode of instruction for language minority students over the past two decades (Gersten, 1985, Bilingual Education Act, 1968); this is to say compensatory—the remedial use of the student's native language while learning the second language. The native language is suddenly eliminated as soon as the students learn the English language. Other types of bilingual programs, such as enrichment of bilingual education, are seldom seen in public schools. In enrichment bilingual programs, children can benefit from learning one or more second languages for psychological, social and economic reasons. According to Fishman and Keller (1982), enrichment of bilingual education is generally asssociated with private and church school efforts. Therefore, when the effects of bilingualism are evaluated in United States, it should be analyzed, taking into consideration this limited type of bilingual education program.

Bilingualism has not been welcomed by the majority of Americans and very little prestige has been attached to having bilingual capacities. According to McLaughlin (1984), in United States, monolingualism traditionally had been the norm and bilingualism had been regarded as a social stigma and a liability. . . . The bilingual represents an alien way of thinking and alien values. It is believed that only 6 percent of the total United States population (Grosjean, 1982) speaks a language other than English on a regular basis. Hakuta (1986) points out that although the United States has probably been host to more bilingual people than any other country in the world, the rate of loss of language diversity in the United States is remarkable when compared with that of other nations. Therefore, when the effects of bilingual education in United States are discussed, these effects have to be seen from the perspective of the limitations of the most popular type of bilingual programs—the compensatory type—in a country that does not value bilingualism as an academically sound instructional program.

Development of Bilingual Proficiency in Children

The process of becoming bilingual is influenced by social and individual factors as well as by language learning contexts. The field of second language acquisition has given emphasis to the role of age in second language learning. Bilingual educators and second language researchers have provided empirical evidence in comparing early language acquirers of different ages in different types of linguistic enrivonments. Theories related to the role of age in second language tends to indicate that the early development of the child maximizes the probability that the younger the human, when exposed to a language, the greater the probability that the individual will acquire a native pronunciation (Asher and Garcia, 1982). There is a belief that the earlier a language is introduced and acquired, the more fluent a person will be in it. These researchers suggest that there are different critical periods for different abilities which determine how completely one can acquire some aspects of language. This popular belief says that youngsters acquire a second language better and foster it better than older acquirers. The critical periods hypothesis, as proposed by Lennenberg (1967), holds that primary language acquisition must occur during a critical period that ends at about the age of puberty with the establishment of cerebral lateralization of function. Lennenberg's (1967) theory is that before the onset of puberty, the brain is more malleable or "plastic" and hence is receptive to such tasks as language learning. Also, young children are said to have fewer inhibitions—less enbarassed when they make mistakes. In other words, it is often argued that the child has a superior biological predisposition to a first language and the young child is thought to acquire a second language easily and quickly. A strong implication of this hypothesis is that the process involved in any language acquisition taking place after the age of puberty will be quantitatively different from those involved in first language acquisition.

But a review of the literature does not indicate a clear positive relationship between age and second language acquisition. McLaughlin (1984) emphatically points out that the evidence does not support this viewpoint. He says the the few studies that have been conducted suggest that older children and adolescents do better than younger children in acquiring a second language in a natural environment. He cites studies conducted by Erwin-Tripp (1974) and Snow and Hoefnagel-Höhle (1978). In recent years, the claim of the age factor has been disputed with several studies (Ekstrand, 1982) apparently showing that older students learn better and quicker. These studies tend to suggest that there is no direct evidence that the child has a special language learning capacity that is absent in the adult (Asher and Garcia, 1969). However, researchers have pointed out that there are some advantages to learning a second language at an early age.

Seliger, Krashen and Ladefoged's (1975) study shows that puberty may be an important turning point in language learning ability. In her review of the literature, Larew (1961) found a consensus that early language learning is preferable. Krashen, Long and Scarcella (1982) say that acquirers who begin natural exposure to a second language during childhood generally achieve higher second language proficiency than those beginning as adults . . . "child second language acquirers will usually be superior in terms of ultimate attainment (younger is better in the long run) (p. 161)." But, they also say that adult and older children in general initially acquire the second language faster than young children (older better for rate of acquisition; younger better for attainment). Their conclusions are in agreement with the results of Asher and Price (1969) Snow and Hoefnagel-Höhle (1978) and Fathman (1975).

Although some of these studies do not prove that there is necessarily a critical period for second language learning, they do suggest that the ability to learn certain aspects of a second language may be age-related. According to Krashen, Long and Scarcella (1979), the available literature is consistent in demostrating that acquirers who begin natural exposure to second languages during childhood generally achieve higher second language proficiency than those beginning as adults. This article is not trying to convince the reader that the learner must be young to become bilingual, nor is it arguing that adults cannot learn a second language. However, evidence is being presented that tend to indicate that there are certain advantages in introducing a second language at early ages. Phonology is not the only advantage, but may involve other aspects such as perception and syntax, although accent is the aspect of second language functioning most often believed to be rather closely age-related.

There seems to be less and less reason to reject the idea that human beings are better able to analyze, integrate and fully utilize a new language if they approach it earlier in life, than if they do so after the early teens. A common claim is that the child is in need of using the language for social interaction and to satisfy basic needs; [Ausubel (1962), Huebner (1979), Jones (1966), McNamara (1966) and Oyama (1975)].

Other researchers theorize that differences in bilingualism or sequential bilingualism are related to learning conditions and not neccesarily to age. A child can become bilingual through simultaneous or sequential bilingualism. On simultaneous bilingualism, the child is exposed to both languages from infancy. The exposure to each language may be personally specific (the father speaks Italian and the mother speaks English or the language spoken at home is Italian and English is spoken in the community). Much of the information we have about simultaneous acquisition comes from diaries kept by parents who brought up their child bilingually, and is most often a one person/one language strategy. The data mostly has been presented in a case-study format. Leopold's (1948) diary study, concerning his daughter Hildegard, is one of them. Hildegard was the offspring of a German linguist father and American mother. Hildegard was introduced at home to German and English. Leopold recorded his daugher's vocalization until she turned eight years old. Leopold reported that Hildegard, at first, did not separate the two languages in her vocabulary, and after three, she used the two languages separately.

In sequential bilingualism, the child obtains some degree of competence in the first language before exposure to the second one. It can happen at an early age when the child starts school, or it can start at a later age. Researchers do not fully agree on whether infant bilinguals go through an initial mixed stage that consists of a single language system containing elements from each language or whether they are able to keep the two languages separate from the onset of language development. Becoming bilingual during pre-school years is often accomplished by interacting with native speakers of the language in the immediate community or in the school setting. Second language acquisition processes involve both transfer and developmental factors. McLaughlin (1984) points out that the child's ultimate bilingualism is not a function of how early a second language is introduced. A child brought up in a bilingual environment from birth may lose that bilingualism when the contact with one of the original languages is lost and the retention of two languages depends on a large number of factors, such as the prestige of cultural pressures, motivation, or opportunities of use, but not on age of acquisition (p. 73). Hakuta (1984) summarizes this conflicting issues by saying:

> There is no evidence for a biologically determined critical period for second-language acquisition, with the possible exception of accent. The developmental patterns of second-language grammar are similar for adults and children. During the initial phase of learning, adults and other children are faster at learning the second language than younger children. In the long run, however, children are more successful learners of a second language. The superiority of children is probably due to attitudinal, motivational, and situational factors rather than to biological factors present only in childhood (p. 232).

Relationship of Bilingualism and Cognitive Development

There has been much debate on the educational and academic effects of bilingualism on the child. Some researchers maintain that bilingualism has negative effects on language development, educational attainment, cognitive growth, and intelligence. Others argue that it has positive effects and that the child is not only ahead in school but has greater cognitive flexibility and creativity (Grosjean, 1982). According to McLaughlin (1984) these arguments can be analyzed from two points of view: "One might predict that two languages are better than one, that a second language gives the child a greater symbolic system and so enhances memory, perception, and creativity; or does a second language interfere with competent cognitive functioning, confusing the child and producing a lack of clarity?" (p. 196). Both arguments have been substantiated in the literature. De Avila and Duncan (1979), suggest that there are certain limitations to both research approaches, especiallly methodological and theoretical confusion (p. 3). It is not the purpose of this article to show how researchers have approached this argument. This article is written under the premise that bilingualism has positive effects on cognitive development. Cognitive development is identified as the mental process by which knowledge is acquired through perception, reasoning and intuition. Several studies have been identified that tend to show the positive relationship between bilingualism and cognitive development, especially before the age of puberty.

The relationship between bilingualism and cognitive abilities has been in the literature for many years. Much of the early literature, especially before the 1960s, was unfavorable toward the positive effects of bilingualism on the development of cognitive skills (Jespersen, 1922; 1948; McNamara, 1966). However, many studies conducted after the 1960s have noted differential and superior performance by bilinguals in a number of cognitive–linguistic areas. Much of the early literature looked at the relationship between bilingualism and intelligence and not on cognitive development. According to Ramirez (1985) these early studies did not consider a number of issues such as "1) relative language proficiency among bilinguals, 2) socio–economic status differences between monolinguals and bilinguals, 3) urban rural differences between monolinguals and bilinguals and; 4) educational opportunites for monolinguals and bilinguals," (p. 194).

Several researchers suggest that there is a positive relationship between bilingualism and cognitive development (Leopold, 1948; Vygosky, 1962; Pearl and Lambert, 1962, and Cummins, 1979). It is suggested that when a group of bilingual individuals are compared with an equivalent group of monolingual individuals in variables such as age, socioeconomic factors, or academic level, with a measure of cognitive flexibility used, bilinguals will do better. And positive effects enable children to use the languages as one particular system and it leads to the development of awareness of linguistic operation. The positive findings are usully associated with majority language groups where the second language is added to the first at no cost to the first. The Pearl and Lambert (1962) study was conducted in six French schools in Montreal, Canada. The subjects included ten-year-old monolingual and bilingual children. Students were tested for degree of bilingualism, by means of both verbal and nonverbal measures of general intelligence (word asociations, detection, picture vocabulary and self-rating-scores). Bilinguals performed significantly higher in intelligence, in both verbal and nonverbal tests. Bilingual children were highly superior in the nonverbal tests. Bilingual children were superior to the monolinguals in concept formation and in tasks that required a certain mental or symbolic flexibility. This study tends to suggest that bilinguals have a diversified intellectual structure and enjoy certain advantages in cognitive flexibity, such as flexibility in thought.

Other studies replicated in some way the Pearl and Lambert study. Cummins (1978) has conducted a number of experiments to determine whether bilingual children have greater conceptual flexibility than do monolingual children. He conducted one study with Irish children looking at the following cognitive tasks: meaning and reference, arbitrariness of language, and non-physical nature of words. Bilingual Irish-English performed higher when compared to monolingual English children. It was Cummins' conclusion that bilingual children surpass monolingual children in conceptual flexibility.

Ben Zeev (1977) reported that monolingual children, aged five to eight, performed more poorly on a symbol substitution task, than Hebrew-English bilingual children. Children were asked to substitute one meaningful word for another in a fixed sentence frame. Ben Zeev concluded that bilinguals develop a more analytical orientation toward language than do monolinguals, as a means of overcoming interference between languages. This study tends to suggest that bilinguals are more aware of the structural similarities and differences between their two languages and develop special sensitivity of linguistic feedback from the environment. Feldman and Sehn (1971) compared bilingual and monolingual subjects on object constancy tasks and found that the bilingual group performed the better tasks. They found that bilingual five-year-old children were better than their monolingual peers at re-labeling objects and using labels in similar relational sentences. Landry (1974) found that sixth-grade children in a foreign language program performed significantly better than monolingual children on a test of divergent thinking ability that measured some aspects of cognitive functioning such as fluency, flexibility, and originality. Balkan (1970) administered several tests of nonverbal abilities to measure cognitive flexibility to monolingual and bilingual 11–17-year-old children. McLaughlin (1984) pointed out that the results were statistically significant for children who had become bilingual before the age of four. For children who had become bilingual later, the results favored the bilinguals but did not reach statistical significance. Bilingual children demonstrated greater cognitive flexibility than their monolingual counterparts in the same series of tests.

Kessler and Quinn (1980) conducted a study with sixth-grade Spanish speakers from Texas. These bilingual students were compared with a group of middle-class monolingual English-speaking students of the same age. Both groups were given an extensive training program in science inquiry through films and discussions of physical science problems and hypothesis testing. In tests given after the training, it was found that the Spanish-English bilinguals generated hypothesis of a much higher quality and complexity than did the monolinguals. Bilinguals were found superior in the quality of hypothesis generated and in scores for written language complexity. Bilinguals had substantially higher scores than monolinguals. The bilingual superiority has been reported in several studies, especially in the area of greater cognitive flexibility, greater creativity and theory, (Ianco-Worral, 1972).

Recent studies have put more emphasis on the aspect of language proficiency. Cummins (1979) has suggested that the type of bilingualism is an important variable in looking at the effects of bilingualism on cognitive and academic development. In his "threshold" hypothesis, if children demonstrate a low level of proficiency in both languages, they are at the threshold of bilingual competence and cognitively and academically effects tend to be negative. He tends to say that for those children that show competence in one language, bilingualism will not produce either positive or negative cognitive effects. In contrast, children who have achieved higher levels of competence in both languages will show positive cognitive effects in the learning and in academic achivement. According to Cummins, "there may be threshold levels of linguistic competence which bilingual children must attain both in order to avoid cognitive deficits and to allow the potentially beneficial aspects of becoming bilingual to influence their cognitive growth (p. 229, cited by McLaughlin, 1984, p. 209). The type of bilingualism may mediate the positive and negative effects of bilingualism on cognitive development. In other words, limited bilingualism results in negative consequences, while proficient bilingualism has positive effects.

Hakuta (1986), outlining a few studies, concludes by saying that bilingualism has little or no influence on general intellectual abilities in childhood. If any effects are to be found at all, these positive effects are in areas closely related to language, such as in metalinguistic abilities. He also says that to the extent that bilingualism is associated with the more prestigious social classes, it correlates positively with measures of intellectual functioning in school (p. 231–232). De Avila and Duncan (1979) hypothesize that "the child who grows up with more than one language, thus acquiring either simultaneously or sequentially two linguistic codes for symbolically manipulating the environment should enjoy an increased metacognitive awareness" (p. 20). Other authors such as Cummins (1978), Blank and Solomon (1968), suggest the possibility that the unique symbolic experiences of the bilingual child may have quite positive consequences and that these children may be potentially intellectually advanced with respect to concept-formation and general mental flexibility.

In summary, there are cognitive advantages related to bilingualism. Swain and Cummins (1971) reviewed most of the recent studies that show the positive effects of bilingualism. They concluded that bilinguals are: a) more sensitive to semantic relations between words, b) more advanced in understanding the arbitrary assignment of names to referents, c) better able to treat sentence structure analytically, d) better at restructuring a perceptual situation, e) more socially sensitive and better able to react more flexibly to cognitive feedback, and f) more divergent in thinking. According to Cummins (1976), the question for research is not what effects does bilingualism, per se, have on cognitive processes, rather research should be directed towards identifying these conditions under which bilingual learning experiences are likely to retard or accelerate aspects of cognitive growth.

Conclusion

Bilingualism has academic implications for bilingual education and second-language instructional programs. Research findings on the relationship between bilingualism and early childhood tend to suggest little positive effects on general intellectual abilities, but they tend to establish a positive relationship on those cognitive abilities directly related to language. These findings allow this writer to conclude that because most of the school activities in the primary grades are language related, then perhaps it is advantageous to introduce children to a second language as early as possible. Learning a second language at an early age does not impede the children's development of the first language. On the contrary, it contributes to the development of metalinguistic abilities, such as semantic relations and analysis of syntactical structures.

References

Asher, J. and Garcia, R. (1969). The optimal age to learn a foreign language. In S. Krashen, R. Scarcella and M. Long (Eds.), *Child adult differences in second-language acquisition*. Rowley, Mass: Newbury House. (pp. 1–19).

Asher J. J. & Price, B. S. (1967). The learning strategy of a total physical response: Some age differences. *Child Development*, *38*, 1219–1227.

Ausubel, D. (1962). Implications of preadolescent and early adolescent cognitive development for secondary-school teaching. *The Modern Language Journal*, *45*, 268–275.

Balkan. L. (1970). *Les effects du bilinguisme francais-anglais sur les aptitudes intellectuelles*. Bruxelles: Aimav.

Ben Zeev, S. (1977). The influence of bilingualism on cognitive strategy and cognitive development. *Child Development*, *48*, 1009–1018.

Bilingual Education Act, 1968. *United Statutes at Large*, vol. 81:817.

Blank, M. & Solomon, F. (1968). A tutorial language program to develop abstract thinking in socially disadvantaged pre-school children. *Child Development*, *39*, 379–389.

Cummins. J. (1980). The cross-lingual dimensions of language proficiency: Implications for bilingual education and the optimal age issue. *TESOL Quarterly*, *14*, 175–87.

Cummins, J. (1979). Linguistic interdependence and the educational development of bilingual children. *Review of Educational Research*, *49*, 221–251.

Cummins, J. (1978). Bilingualism and the development of metalinguistic awareness. *Journal of Cross-Cultural Psychology*, *9*, 139–149.

Cummins, J. (1976). The influence of bilingualism on cognitive growth: A synthesis of research findings and explanatory hypotheses. *Working Papers on Bilingualism*, *9*, 1–9.

De Avila E. A. & Duncan S. E. (Winter, 1979). Bilingualism and the metaset. *NABE Journal*, *3*(2), 1–20.

Diaz, R. (1983). Thought and two languages: The impact of bilingualism on cognitive development. *Review of Research in Education*, *10*, 23–54.

Ekstrand, L. H. (1982). English without a book revisited: The effect of age in second language acquisition in a formal setting. In Krashen S., R. Scarcella and M. Long (Eds.), *Child–adult differences in second language acquisition*. Rowley, Mass: Newbury House.

Ekstrand, L. H. (1979). Replacing the critical period and optimun age theories of second language acquisiton with a theory of ontogenetic development beyond puberty. *Educational and Psychological Interactions*. (Malmö, Sweden: School of Education), *69*.

Erwin-Tripp, S. (1974). Is second-language learning like the first? *TESOL Quarterly*, *8*, 111–127.

Fathman, A. (1975). The relationship between age and second-language productive ability. *Language Learning, 25,* 245–253.

Fathman A. (1975). Language backgrounds, age, and the order of English structures. Paper presented at the TESOL Convention, Los Angeles, California.

Feldman, C. & Sehn, M. (1971). Some language-related cognitive advantages of bilingual 5-year olds. *Journal of Genetic Psychology, 118,* 235–244.

Fishman, J. A. & Keller G. D. (1982). *Bilingual education for Hispanic students in the United States.* New York: Teachers College Press, Columbia University.

Gersten, R. (1985). Structured immersion for language minority students: Results of a longitudinal evaluation. *Educational Evaluation and Policy Analysis, 7*(3), 187–196.

Crosjean, F. (1982). *Life with two languages.* Cambridge, Mass.: Harvard University Press.

Hakuta, K. (1986). *Mirror of language.* New York: Basic Books.

Huebener, T. (1979). Order of acquisition vs. dynamic paradigm: A comparison of methods in interlanguage research. *TESOL Quarterly, 13,* 21–28.

Ianco-Worral, A. (1972). Bilingualism and cognitive development. *Child Development, 43,* 1390–1400.

Jespersen, O. (1964). *Language, its nature, development and origin.* New York: H. Holt & Co. (1928) (Original edition, 1922).

Jones, W. R. (1966). *Bilingualism in Welsh education.* Cardiff: University of Wales Press.

Kessler, C. & Quinn. (1980). Positive effects of bilingualism on science problem-solving abilities. In J. E. Alatis (Ed.), *Current issues in bilingual education.* Washington, D.C.: Georgetown University Press.

Krashen, S. Long, M. & Scarcella R. (1979). Age, rate and attainment in second-language acquisition. *TESOL Quarterly, 13,* 573–582.

Landry, R. G. (1974). A comparison of second-language learners and monolinguals on divergent thinking tasks at the elementary school level. *Modern Language Journal, 58,* 10–15.

Larew, L. (1961). The optimun age for beginning a foreign language. *Modern Foreign Language, 45,* 203–206.

Lennerberg, E. (1967). *Biological foundations of language.* New York: Wiley.

Leopold, W. F. (1948). The study of child language and infant bilingualism. *Word, 4,* 1–17.

McLaughlin, B. (1984). *Second language acquisition in childhood.* Hillsdale, N.J.: Erlbaum.

McNamara, J. (1966). *Bilingualism and primary education.* Edinburgh: Edinburgh University Press.

Oyama, S. (1976). A sensitive period for the acquisition of a nonnative phonological system. *Journal of Psycholinguistic Research, 5,* 262–285.

Pearl, E. and Lambert, W. E. (1962). The relation of bilingualism to intelligence. *Psychological Monographs, 76* (27, whole no. 546).

Ramirez, A. (1985). *Bilingualism through schooling.* Albany: State University of New York Press.

Seliger, H., Krashen S. & Ladefoged, P. (1975). Maturational constraints in the acquisition of second language accent. *Language Sciences, 36,* 20–22.

Snow, C. & Hoefnagel-Höhle, M. (1978). The critical period for language acquisition: Evidence from second-language learning. *Child Development, 49*, 114–28.
Swain, M. & Cummins, J. (1979). Bilingualism, cognitive functioning and education: Language Teaching and Linguistics: *Abstracts, 12*, 4–18.
Vygotsky, L. S. (1962). *Thought and language*. Cambridge, Mass: MIT Press.

Chapter 9

Content-Rich Day-Care Centers

Marjorie Grosett

Day Care Council of New York

As teachers, we all understand the need in any early childhood program to provide children with a range of planned experiences designed to foster language development, reading readiness, numerical and spatial concepts. We also need to provide opportunities for artistic expression and to help them develop hand–eye coordination and fine-finger control. As well, we strive to give them an appreciation of their cultural heritage and our national mores.

If we start with these as desirable goals for young children, and if all your previous experience has been with nursery schools, public schools, early childhood programs and similar operations, you must then consider how differently those basic principles must be applied to the long-day program offered in a day-care facility. What is the difference? Let's start with the definition of day care, which alone will explain what is different about it.

Day-Care Program Goals

Day care has sometimes been described as a child welfare service which functions in an educational setting. The emphasis, however, is on child welfare even though early childhood education is an important component of the program.

The vast increase of mothers in the work force, together with the alarming rise in family problems generally, has caused a corresponding increase in the need for day care as an all-day, year-round service designed first to provide support to parents, with education for their children a close second priority. School-based early childhood and nursery programs operate for no more than 3 to 5 hours daily and they close in summer and on all public holidays, whether major or minor. Day-care centers, on the other hand, are in business primarily to serve the children of parents who are employed full time, outside the home, usually from 9 a.m. to 5 p.m., and who need child care not only for those hours but also for an additional hour or more at the beginning and end of each workday to allow for travel between home and job. This means that most day-care centers operate at least 10 hours per day, usually from 8 a.m. to 6 p.m., remain open throughout the summer and close for no more than 10 or 11 holidays per year. In short, these centers must be prepared to care for children whenever their parents work. In some communities, this may even mean that the center must provide child care during evening hours or on weekends. Most notably, programs serving the children of hospital employees and evening session college students frequently operate on such varied schedules.

This nontraditional scheduling obviously has some clear implications for the kinds of program for children which the center must plan and implement during the long, 10-hour day. In New York, where the day-care network is very large, the majority of our centers serve preschoolers between the ages of 3 and 6. At age 6, New York centers graduate their children to the first grade of the nearby public school. Because the city licensing code requires every day-care classroom to be headed by a graduate teacher who is state-certified, a 5-year-old child's attendance in the classroom qualifies as kindergarten experience, thus permitting automatic entry to first grade.

Thus, the ages of these children as well as the long program day, spanning 10 or more hours, present serious challenges to all program planners in the way in which they apply the basic child development principles.

Staff Requirements

In the first instance, these factors affect the kind of staffing and staff schedules which a program must have. Let's face it, not one of us or any teacher known to us would be willing to work a 10-hour day with such young children. But the fact is, many children do attend the center and need service for that number of hours. Because of that, staff in day-care centers must be increased in number, perhaps three times as many as would be required to staff a public school kindergarten serving the same number of children. A school-based kindergarten, for example, would probably be staffed with a single teacher who, in turn, might be assisted by a part-time aide, though not always. The same number of children in a 10-hour day-care classroom would require three adults, one of whom must be a certified teacher. Those three adults would be scheduled to work in staggered, overlapping shifts in order to cover the long day, so that when the first teacher goes home, the second and third members of the team will still be available to the children. Teachers, of course, must arrive at different times, as well as leave at different times. Careful scheduling is required, not only for the hours of work of the classroom staff but also for the times of the day when children are to be involved in cognitive developmental activities, as opposed to vigorous outdoor play, or periods of rest and quiet relaxation.

To reduce the stress of that long day, it is recommended that staff work with children in small groups and that they plan to alternate active periods with periods of close intensive work, interspersed liberally with quiet times for storytelling or music listening. Fatigue is the greatest enemy of good, satisfying programming. With fatigue comes a number of other problems. Children become overstimulated, overtired, fretful and aggressive. Teachers will have problems of discipline and management while the potential for accidents rises. Staff in turn will be placed under stress. Thus, the very best, most ingenious efforts are called for in planning the everyday program schedules for the activities of children under these conditions.

Who Needs Day Care?

We begin by talking about day care as a service to parents who are employed full time and need child care while they work. Teachers should also be aware, however, that there are others who may or may not work who also need and use day care for their children. For example, we are all aware of the growing problem of teen-age pregnancy, and the fact that an alarming number of adolescents are finding themselves responsible for the care of an infant before they have developed the needed life skills. For these teen-age parents, day care offers some limited solutions. They are limited for several reasons, not immediately controllable, but which we hope will be addressed in the near future. Specifically, very few day-care centers provide care for infants or toddlers. When they do, their cost is far outside the ability of teen-age parents to meet. Publicly subsidized programs which might provide free or low-cost service for infants are even fewer in number. For this reason, we are finding that many of the girls in question become overwhelmed and sometimes abandon their babies or turn them over for care by their own mothers. Thus, our centers are experiencing increased enrollments of children whose grandmothers have had to assume responsibility for their care. That grandmother is usually a middle-aged lady, still working, who has already raised a family, and who was not expecting to assume responsibility for a new set of young children at this stage of her life. Sometimes in these situations we find that the teen-age mother may be seriously troubled, may or may not be still in the parental home, may be drug-addicted, a runaway, or even incarcerated.

My organization, the Day Care Council of New York, is an umbrella organization providing services to its member day-care programs which are designed to help them serve children better. One of the Council's recent service programs was designed to reestablish linkages between certain children in day care and their mothers who were incarcerated at Riker's Island. The number of these is relatively small, but the problems are acute. Council staff meets and works with young mothers who are in the Women's House of Detention, as well as grandmothers or other relatives who may be at home with the children. Parenting seminars are provided for the mothers at Riker's to help them assume and cope with their child-rearing responsibilities when they return home. Prison walls literally provide a captive audience for such instruction; those outside seldom receive this same kind of help while still at home with their children.

Though these are extreme examples, it should nevertheless be obvious that a program serving children from these and similarly troubled backgrounds must offer more than just the traditional early childhood education activities. Parents and children may both be in need of social work or other counseling, and the day-care center must be prepared to make knowledgeable referrals, when necessary, to such other services as mental health and medical care and even to agencies providing assistance with welfare and housing needs.

Day Care for Infants

Despite this grim picture, the growing demand we see for day-care programs serving infants does not come primarily from troubled families and teen-age parents. On the contrary, the bulk of this demand is coming from higher-income women in stable family situations who are finding it necessary to return to work earlier and earlier after childbirth. We note that the average maternity leave for women in the business world has now shrunk to less than 6 months, at which point they begin seeking care for their infant children so that they can return to work. It should be noted here that educated career women are not satisfied to accept mere custodial care, however loving, for their infants. They expect that early childhood educators will, by now, have developed a curriculum of intellectually stimulating activities specifically for infants. It is doubtful that we have developed all of the concepts of appropriate activities for infants that we can, even though programs exist which claim to do so.

Day Care in Private Homes: "Family Day Care"

It is clear that the few infant programs that do exist are not nearly enough to meet this serious growing demand. It is for that reason that the majority of care for infants whose mothers work is given either in the child's own home or in the home of someone the parents describe as a "baby-sitter." Parental fears about this kind of care are legion and many of our established child welfare and educational agencies have established networks of supervised homes called *family day-care* programs. A family day-care program is one in which a number of homes are attached administratively to a responsible child-caring agency so that children can be referred, and training and supervision assured in each participating day-care home. The agency which is responsible for operating the program assumes responsibility for recruiting interested caregivers, screening them and their homes, interviewing their families and arranging, upon acceptance, to provide the prospective caregiver with some child development training and some child-related equipment as needed to care for the children who will be assigned. The home is then licensed and subject to regular monitoring visits as well as ongoing educational seminars for the caregiver. Lending libraries for toys and educational materials help round out the resources of each home.

State regulations limit the children each home can accept to a maximum of six, including the caregiver's own children. The supports offered to the caregiver by the operating agency include seminars on age-appropriate activities for children of varied ages, as well as the provision of special materials and equipment, as needed. These might include some small tables and chairs, a high chair, a stroller, or a folding crib. Even in this more flexible environment, service to infants is limited to a maximum of two to a home for safety reasons. A truly skilled and vigilant operating agency is required to ensure that the quality of the program in each home does not deteriorate to "electronic baby-sitting," that is, the practice of seating the children in front of the TV set all day long to free the caregiver to do other things. Thus a competent operating agency must also help the caregiver develop a schedule of appropriate activities with the children, including trips outdoors, as well as the management of his or her own household activities in ways that will enable him or her to get the housework done, prepare the family's evening meal before her spouse's return from work, and still provide interesting activities and adequate care for the children during the course of the day.

To ensure that all this happens, the operating agency will provide a monitor, who visits the home on a regular basis to bring materials, assess progress, and provide general help. The book and toy exchange library helps ensure that continued interest and variation in the materials are made available to children. After the preservice training, additional seminars for caregivers are usually conducted monthly and cover a host of issues related to child development and the handling of problem situations among the children. Caregivers are not salaried; they are paid a weekly fee for each child they accept for care. In some instances, these family day-care networks are attached to existing day-care centers as a means of serving older and younger siblings in the same family and sharing the training and staff resources offered by the day-care center with the caregivers in the satellite homes. In this arrangement, the preschool children, aged 3 to 6, are usually in attendance at the day-care center while their older or younger siblings are assigned to one of the nearby homes. Younger children graduate from the home to the center with school-age children leaving the center to attend a home, part time, in the after-school hours. Programs like these are the most flexible response thus far that early childhood specialists have been able to make to the rising need for programs serving infants. Much more, however, is required.

As stated earlier, the principal cause of the lack of growth in programs for infants is the proportionately higher cost of group care programs for babies. We've already noted the fact that a kindergarten class of 20 children would require three full-time staff members to cover the long program day in a day-care center. If infants were substituted for kindergarteners, more than one classroom would be required for the same number of children and the ratio of staff to infants would be one adult for every 4 babies or a total of five full-time staff members to care for 20 infants. That, of course, increases costs enormously and accounts, at least in part, for the widespread resistance to the development of day-care centers serving infants. Further, many child development experts oppose the care of infants in groups on the ground that such young children require the one-to-one nurturing only possible in a home environment. This probably means that the real challenge to early childhood educators is to find ways to enrich the home care environment to include as many components of good early childhood programming as possible, remembering that these programs must utilize individuals who are not professional teachers and who still have to answer the needs of running a home while providing the high-quality care and education we strive for.

After-School Care

In addition to the need to develop more programs serving infants, an enormous need also exists to provide programs for the many thousands of young schoolchildren who are dismissed from school at 3 p.m. when their parents are still at work. These children return each day alone to an empty house to spend hours without supervision or constructive activity. Because of the house key entrusted to them by the working parent, they are commonly called "latchkey" children. Each year, hundreds fall victim to gang violence, sexual abuse, and drugs during these unsupervised, unprotected hours. Many programs which claim to offer services to this population provide little more than a program of sports or other recreation which children may attend or not as they please. Parents need and want a great deal more. Parents want genuine supervision which includes taking attendance on arrival, and dismissal to a designated adult at a specified time. Parents also want a real educational program, designed to provide opportunities for the child to build upon the curriculum of the school in ways that are less formal and more enjoyable, in ways that provide opportunities for creative and artistic expression, cultural enrichment, and hobby skills and under certain circumstances, even homework supervision is provided.

The skills of early childhood educators must also be challenged to develop this kind of curriculum to complement the traditional one for young schoolchildren.

Industry-Related Day Care

In considering the rising demand for early childhood services, we find that employers, especially large corporations, have also begun to be concerned about their employees' child-care needs and the impact this has on everyday work performance. Many employers have established child-care information and referral systems to help parents find suitable programs in their home communities; others have offered stipends or vouchers to help parents defray their child-care costs, but some have taken the giant step of establishing a child-care center of their own at or near the work site. In New York City, this occurs primarily with hospitals, some of which have established day-care centers for their employees.

For example, the Day Care Council has been heavily involved for the past year in working with a group of hospitals anxious to develop child-care services for their medical personnel, primarily nurses, but for support staff as well, all of whom need child care during the nontraditional hours of hospital operation. A hospital, after all, is a 24-hour, 7-day-a-week operation. Parents/employees may work nights, weekends, and holidays and need child care at all these times. We have helped several hospitals to develop child-care services. One has developed a network of family day-care homes. Another has opened its own day-care center near the hospital. A third has joined with another nearby hospital to establish a day-care center for the children of both hospitals' employees.

Another group of institutions, similar yet different from hospitals, is large urban colleges. Again, as we look at all the societal changes in the way we work, study, marry, and have children, we must recognize that colleges are affected by these changes to the same extent as all other institutions. We are finding that today's college students differ from the traditional postadolescent group. Many are mature students who have decided to return to school after a few years in the work force or after marriage or military service, and who are now starting a family. Like the parents with full-time jobs, these are also people who have families and who need child care while they study and, often, also while they work. As a result, we have also consulted with several colleges to help them open child-care programs on the premises of the college.

These are unique, nontraditional programs with strong educational resources. They don't operate from 8 a.m. to 6 p.m. but more often from 7 a.m. to 10 p.m. That doesn't mean that any one child spends all those hours there. The children appear at the center in staggered shifts, and not necessarily for 5 consecutive days. Students may have class schedules requiring attendance on Tuesday, Thursday, and Friday, for example, and those are the days on which their children will attend the center. On one day they may have morning classes; on another day they may have all-day classes. In addition, there is another whole body of evening session students whose children may attend from late afternoon until 10 p.m. Colleges do not operate on Saturdays, Sundays, and holidays as hospital programs do, but the programming challenges are just as great. A college-based program, however, is able to draw upon the educational resources of its parent institution to create a living laboratory for the development of new curriculum concepts. Few others are so lucky.

Family Needs and Educational Goals

All of this means that the emphasis now has to be on rethinking the needs of the children we educate. Emphasis must now be on structuring the same principles that we've already agreed should be common to all early childhood programs into new and innovative systems. We need to structure and repackage them in ways that can function creatively in these varied and diversified settings that I have described. It means also that as teachers we're going to have to become quasi-social workers in ways that we never expected and for which we have had no training. The emphases on the family, as well as on the changing structure and needs of each family, are going to change the educational and social needs of each child that we as educators have responsibility for. This means that universities and schools of education must begin to prepare teachers to cope with the new demands of the profession. It entails a thorough assessment of the children we are responsible for or likely to serve, putting together profiles of families and deciding, based on the knowledge and information that we have, how best to structure a program that will contain the basic ingredients of early learning but is presented in a way that will have meaning and value to them.

Some of our day-care centers are regularly serving children from some very disturbed backgrounds. Do not assume, however, that because our publicly funded day-care centers serve primarily the children of poor working families that this is a phenomenon limited to the poor. This is assuredly not the case. The social problems that parents and children are facing in suburbia as well as the inner city are not limited to any one economic or ethnic group. Never start with that premise or you will be defeated at once. We all know that many of the problems teachers report that children manifest in the classroom can be traced directly to very disturbed situations at home. Planning is more successful if one takes the trouble to assess potential problems first. The second thing you must do is to make an early assessment of each child's functioning. Be aware that there is an acute rise in health problems, some of these related to housing problems. It is important to bear in mind that teachers are mandated by law to report any signs of child abuse that they observe. You don't have to know for sure that it happened and the law protects you from reprisals, and preserves your anonymity. There are penalties if you fail to report your suspicions for investigation. Those penalties are levied if some injury befalls a child after you observed that there were symptoms of abuse and neglect and failed to report them.

All of these factors now make the job of teaching young children much more challenging than it used to be. I hope that we can look forward to greatly expanded teacher education programs in the colleges as well as a willingness on the part of more young teachers to the challenges I have just described. Today's children need you desperately. [Note: The foregoing material was originally presented at a seminar for graduate teachers. Tho questions and answers which follow therefore, represent the dialogue that ensued between seminar participants and the presenter.]

Questions and Answers

Question: *Is there a standardized curriculum for day-care centers?*

Answer: *No. Curriculum is always developed by the individual teachers to meet the needs of each particular group of children, as it should be. Of course, state and city regulations do require that each program include such basic components as activities to foster children's language development, artistic expression, math and science concepts, and so forth. But development of an individualized curriculum is the responsibility of each teacher who, we hope, will base his or her learning plans on an assessment of the specific needs of the children in her care.*

Question: *Can family day-care providers have as many as 6 children, even in very small apartments?*

Answer: *I said that a mother cannot have more than six children including her own but if, when her home is inspected, it's determined that she simply doesn't have the physical space to accommodate that many children, she can't have that many.*

Question: *Is space the only consideration in determining whether the environment of a home is suitable for day-care purposes?*

Answer: *What is considered in the environment of the home concerns not only the physical layout but also the people in it—their habits, their attitudes, their feelings about having children in their homes. If you have a mother who is anxious to become a day-care provider, but find that her husband is outraged at the possibility that he may arrive home at the end of his working day and find some of the children still present, then that home environment is not conducive to development of a good day-care home. No responsible agency would certify such a home. In addition, there may be physical problems in the home itself. Certainly, we would insist, for example, that every room have window guards. Again, many apartments do not, and that would be part of the equipment that an agency would help them provide or install, assuming all other items were acceptable.*

Question *Do you really have sufficient personnel to visit all the little home centers?*

Answer: *That's a very perceptive question and the answer is critical to maintaining quality standards in all home-based programs. Our member agencies in the Day Care Council include family day-care agencies of three types. One class consists of professional social work agencies which operate family day-care networks in conjunction with social work counseling and sometimes foster-care services. In these homes are enrolled children whose parents are usually in need of special counseling. Because the heavy emphasis of these agencies is on social work, they do have the staff to visit these homes frequently as well as to counsel parents and children.*

Another class of family day-care agencies is called Family Day Care Careers programs. The name is misleading nowadays but came about when the program first began because originally it offered career training and employment guidance to mothers who enrolled their children. It also provided training of the home-care providers to help them upgrade their skills to the point where they might eventually find employment in a day-care center or nursery school. Though the program no longer has this career component, it still does provide training for caregivers and has sufficient staff to make the needed supervisory and monitoring visits on a regular basis. The third group of home-care network agencies consists of those which are attached to nearby day-care centers, and homes are thus enabled to share training and other resources with the staff of the center.

Despite the quality of these professional operations, it is important to remember that family day care or child care in private homes has been the oldest and most widely used form of child care in every society throughout history. The woman down the street who undertakes to "baby-sit," the nice neighbor next door or other friend who agrees, for a fee, to care for the children while mother works; these have always been the traditional family day-care providers who make individual and private arrangements with the families they serve. The concept of supervising such a home and providing training and support to that "baby-sitter" through affiliation with a professional agency is a new and sometimes unwelcome idea to these independent caregivers. Such a caregiver may or may not choose to apply to the local authorities for a license, since in doing so, someone will visit his or her home and make an assessment of its suitability. Even assuming that they do apply for and obtain a license, it is most unlikely that any follow-up visits will ever be made after the first evaluating visit during the 1 or 2 years that the license remains in effect, until renewed. For this reason, there is nearly no control over private individuals who decide to "baby-sit" children in their homes. Indeed, nothing can be done unless a complaint is made about the handling of a particular child or children. Few complaints are made, but when they are, they are often serious.

I can remember one telephone call I received in the late afternoon from a distraught mother who had just returned home after picking up her 4-year-old from the baby-sitter, who lived in the same apartment building. After the child's complaint and her examination of the child, the mother came to the conclusion that the child had been sexually molested. It was her belief that the baby-sitter's teen-age son was responsible. I suggested that she seek immediate medical attention for the child and report the matter to the police. The mother became hysterical at this suggestion since because the baby-sitter was her neighbor, and the molester the neighbor's son, she, the mother, was fearful of the consequences if she followed my advice. I then suggested that she talk to her private doctor and, tomorrow morning, go and register her child at the neighborhood day-care center so that, at least, her child would not have to return to the baby-sitter's home. It was urgent that she make immediate alternative arrangements. Finally, I asked the mother her name. Her fright immediately returned and she expressed the fear that if I knew her name I would report the matter to the police myself, and she promptly hung up.

This incident only serves to illustrate the fact that there is virtually no control or supervision over these independent caregivers. Parents can only be urged to make the best possible choices and, to the extent possible, at least seek out those independent caregivers who were interested enough to apply for a family day-care home license. The license, at least, guarantees that the initial basic standards have been met with respect to safety and character of the caregiver and her family. To help parents with these choices, several organizations have developed some basic checklists which parents can use in making their own assessments of a potential caregiver's home and standards. Finally, we urge parents to sit down with potential caregivers at the start of their relationship and come to a clear understanding about their own expectations for the standards of care.

Question: *Do day-care centers serve handicapped children?*

Answer: *Not in any substantial number, but the answer is yes. For the most part, children with special needs but not severe handicaps are mainstreamed into the regular classroom. There are a few centers, however, which have special classrooms for children whose handicaps make it impossible for them to be part of the mainstream classroom environment.*

Question: *Are children from troubled backgrounds usually tied to certain communities? And do they have the same abilities as other children in their age group?*

Answer: *I would have to say yes, I think that such families have limited mobility and are therefore more likely to be found in certain neighborhoods, though not necessarily. The children, however, often show more independence, and sometimes greater language facility. Of course, teachers may not like what they say since, in some communities, children may be skilled enough to know bad words in more than one language. But they are nevertheless quite verbal and articulate. It is teachers who must face the challenge of channeling that ability into constructive advantageous activities. In addition, it has often been noted that children from seriously troubled backgrounds are less likely to consider the needs of others or to engage in teamwork. Teachers should make use of those games and activities that are specifically designed to engender team cooperation among the players. These include activities that one child cannot accomplish alone so has to work together with a friend in order to accomplish the task or play the game.*

A major goal in a day-care center, of course, is the socialization of children, and that includes concepts of sharing, attention and consideration for the wants of others in relation to oneself. One of the earliest lessons any child must learn is that he or she must hold one's fists and not lash out and punch or strike the child next to him or her because he or she has a wanted toy. As children grow older, they must also learn to hold their tongues and not express everything they think, which is another means of hurting others. This is part of everyone's developmental process and we as adults certainly know, as we advance in our jobs, careers, families, and social circles, that we must control our speech to the same extent as our fists. This only means that the socializing process for children must begin at the earliest stages and teachers have major responsibility for contributing positively to the process.

As we read newspapers every day, much of what we see and hear has to do with the way parents rear children. Parents must cope with street influences outside the home, as well as influences of older siblings and friends inside the home. We are living in a climate of violence, helped in part by some television offerings and some of the lyrics of current popular music. These do not teach children to cooperate or to respect others, the rights of others or themselves.

Unless teachers accept responsibility for counteracting some of these influences in the classroom, all of society will face increasing problems as these little ones grow up.

Question: *How can teachers handle individual children who are especially disruptive and who may hurt others?*

Answer: *Generally we have encouraged teachers to develop special activities, based on the assessment of the child's needs and to identify one or two of those activities which seem to interest him or her more than others. Day-care centers are fortunate to have more than one staff member at a time in each classroom. This will enable the teacher to assign an aide or assistant to work with a disruptive child on a one-to-one basis, to help him or her develop some interest which later can be used to help him work back into the larger group.*

One of the things we've learned is that being in a classroom all day with 20 children can be stressful for children and adults alike. In addition, we have also learned that many of the children who manifest problems may live in crowded household situations which afford them little privacy or time for quiet play and reflection.

Being in a large day-care classroom with 20 children simply adds to the stress which they may have carried over from the home. This is one of the reasons why, in planning classroom furniture arrangements, teachers must arrange to provide a quiet sheltered corner where children can retreat from the "crowd" to sit quietly and watch the fish in the tank or read books, play with small table toys, and generally have some privacy. Teachers should not only encourage these opportunities but should also plan to work with children in small groups, utilizing the assistant teacher or aides who may be present, so that children can have a "fair share" of each of the caring adults in that classroom. This technique has been especially successful with the kind of children we've been talking about. In some of these situations, we have sometimes found that Monday morning can be the worst day of the teacher's week because the child comes fresh from a whole weekend of whatever environment has been disturbing him or her. Teachers need to plan special activities for these occasions and to utilize all the resources that the center may have to offer.

Question: *Are school-based prekindergarten programs likely to have an impact on day-care enrollment?*

Answer: *The answer to that is yes and no. It depends on the community, nearness of the school to the day-care center and so on. Money and day-care charges are also a factor. We had a very sad situation last year in which a number of day-care parents withdrew their children from the center to enroll them in the "free" all-day kindergarten advertised by the nearby school. Sadly, they learned that what the schools call "all-day" is a program which operates from 9 a.m. to 2:30 p.m., while the words "all-day" in a day-care center mean 8 a.m. to 6 p.m. Parents were shocked to discover that their children would not be cared for until they returned from work. In publicly funded day-care programs, which are very numerous here in New York, parents' fees are charged on a sliding scale, based on the family's income. But to a poor family, even $5 or $6 per week looks like an unnecessary burden when the school down the street is offering what seems to be the same service free of charge. Despite this, there were several instances in which some of these parents came back to the day-care center and tried to reregister their children for the long-day service they needed. Unfortunately, their children had usually been replaced by others who needed long-day service, so re-enrollment was not possible.*

I did note earlier that a few day-care centers offer after-school service and that service is usually for children aged 6 to 9. Until recently there had been no demand for after-school service for 5-year-olds who are dismissed at 2:30 p.m. from kindergarten classes. And day-care centers have been reluctant to offer such part-day service to this age group, partly because they already offer full-day service to the same ages and partly because they are limited by their operating licenses to service a specified number of children. They therefore cannot suddenly open their doors to 20 or 40 more 5-year-olds, for which they are not licensed. In some instances, service to this group would mean discontinuing service to another group of children, perhaps at the 8- to 9-year-old level in order to make room for these younger ones. These are not easy choices for centers to make, so they must assess the full range of needs in their community and then address what seems to be the predominant, majority need which will serve the maximum number of children.

Question: *Is industry really showing interest in providing day-care assistance to their employees?*

Answer: *Yes. Particularly hospitals, which are concerned about the national shortage of nurses. Many of them believe that opening a child-care service is a significant tool for recruitment, and in some instances that does seem to work. But among nonhospital employers, especially those in the metropolitan area, there is limited interest in actually developing an on-site day-care service. Instead, there is a growing trend among employers to offer some kind of family support to their employees, whether it involves assistance to children, elderly parents, or other family needs. This did not come about by accident, of course, but rather because the same problems we've been discussing that affect poor children in day-care centers are affecting some affluent, professional families as well. That, in turn, affects the performance of those employees on the job. Since the problem is not limited to women or affected solely by child-care needs, employers are now offering such services as social work, marital, and financial counseling to counteract some serious family disruptions which spill over into the workplace.*

As an example, yesterday an attorney who is a senior partner in a large prestigious law firm told me that he had dismissed from his firm a young man of brilliant background and promise who, they discovered, had begun to embezzle funds from one of the trusts for which the firm was responsible. He was married, was supporting a mistress and a costly cocaine habit. And though this incident may sound like a soap opera, the fact is that drug abuse is not limited to poor families living in the ghetto. I am told that Wall Street abounds with cocaine sellers who are stationed at the curb throughout the lunch hour to sell their wares to the young executives who then go back to their offices to handle your money and mine. Corporations are understandably increasingly concerned about problems of this kind and they are taking steps, not only to eliminate abuses, but also to institute services which may help prevent individuals from becoming entrapped in the first place.

The growing number of divorces in middle-income families has sometimes left the father, rather than the mother, as the parent with sole responsibility for the child or children. Child care for such a father is so urgent as to become a concern of his employer as well as himself. Corporations are also aware of the growing number of situations in which a middle-aged executive may have an aged parent who is ill and must be given care at home. And the cost of that care may bankrupt the family. Similarly, the cost of care for a retarded or handicapped child may also bankrupt the family emotionally as well as financially. Corporations are finding that they must provide help of some kind in these situations or they can't get the best performance from an otherwise valued employee. For all these reasons, employers have begun to institute family support services which provided needed counseling as well as financial stipends or various kinds of help with child care, elder care, drug and alcohol addiction services and even legal defense services at times. This last has come about because of situations in which the teen-age child of some corporate executive has faced arrest and prosecution and the distraught parent cannot function in his professional capacity without outside help.

Question: *You know, you have been giving us a different view from that of previous speakers. In general they have been telling us that school should strive to be more like the family. But obviously these speakers had good families. I know a few cases where the school is actually a reprieve from the family. I'm wondering if we are lacking in vision if we don't recognize that something has gone wrong with the family, through stress and strain, when we have a child from a troubled home. And because we have the child for 10 hours a day, isn't it possible that we could do much more to prevent future crime and violence if we were a little more visionary about our early child care?*

Answer: *There's a lot of evidence to support that, of course. The Ypsilanti study which has followed a group of former preschool children for nearly 20 years, has now shown that those children who had the benefit of a good solid foundation in a quality early childhood program have come through with flying colors. The collected data of the study showed only a tiny percentage of the preschool program graduates succumbed to such social pathologies as drug abuse, adolescent pregnancy or other undesirable activities. It is important to note that these children all came from the same deprived environment as others in the study who fared far less well and who did not participate in the preschool program. But we as educators have always believed that good early childhood programs can make a positive difference in children's development and attitudes.*

Nevertheless, we must be aware that the general environment is changing, there are influences among children that we are going to have to think hard about counteracting. Some of these influences, unfortunately, are coming from the home. The title of this series, "The Family in the Schools," means that schools are going to have to pay more and more attention to what is happening in the family and find ways to work with the family as well as the child. We cannot continue to see and treat the child as an isolated entity. We've got to see him or her in his or her total environment which includes the entire cast of characters that constitutes his or her family or household. We all know that families can no longer be defined as consisting of mother, father, and 2.5 children. We now know that whatever people, arrangements, and relationships form a child's home circle constitute the family. We must learn to respect and work with whatever form the family takes.

Question: *Do day-care centers have PTAs, or call parent-teacher conferences?*

Answer: *A good teacher does plan regular parent conferences. Every center is required to have a PAC, that is, the parent advisory committee. But it is a committee; it is not the body of parents as a whole. The center will probably also convene meetings of the whole body of parents two or three times a year. However, that is really not the way in which you are going to obtain their participation in program planning. One of the major differences between day care and Head Start, for example, is the fact that day-care parents work. Each parent has a full-time job, so may not appreciate requests to come into the school during working hours to go over your plans for his or her child. In addition to that, they often live in neighborhoods in which people are afraid to go out at night. And so, if you call a parents meeting for 8 p.m., nobody will come. Again, teachers must look at where they are and what people will find sensible. For that reason, we have learned a number of variations which do obtain parent participation.*

In general we urge our centers to plan meetings for 5 p.m. since parents generally arrive between 5 and 6 p.m. to pick up their children after work. Thus, if teachers plan the meeting at that time, offer parents some refreshment, and continue to provide child care while the meeting is in session, they will stay. They will meet and discuss with you, and give you the opportunity to communicate some of your goals and expectations for their children. And you in turn will be able to learn, and it's important to do so, what parents' aspirations are for their children. New York is a very ethnically diverse city and one of the lessons we've learned is that different ethnic groups not only have different child-rearing practices but also different expectations for their children. It's wise to find out what those are before you blunder in and make some inappropriate demands, or insist on teaching a child something his or her parents may actually consider disrespectful. However, in addition to knowing what parents desire, you as a professional educator, need to interpret to parents our reasons for doing some of the things we do, and what reasonable expectations for a child's development and learning ought to be. That's your area of expertise and it's your job to share and interpret that. It's not uncommon, for example, for parents from certain ethnic groups to come into the day-care center and demand that their 3-year-olds be taught to read. Especially since they believe that the public school isn't doing a very good job of this, they strongly hope that the day-care center will begin to take care of it, now, while the child is 3 years old.

Question: *What do you tell that parent?*

Answer: *You explain why 3-year-olds are not developmentally "ready" to begin formal reading instruction. But as a professional educator, you have to be prepared to cope with unrealistic expectations like that. This means providing parents with a sensitive interpretation of the developmental capacities of children at various age levels. It also means providing parents with the reassurance they need that the center will indeed, through its planned curriculum, provide ample opportunities for children to develop the desired reading readiness skills and related abilities which are needed for later school success.*

Question: *Just a decade ago, there were a lot of child development labs where children could be exposed to special intensive learning situations and teachers could observe patterns of children's growth. Are these lessening?*

Answer: *Well, of course. They are almost entirely out of business due to cuts in federal funds. Almost all of them were federally funded, and as you know, federal dollars for research of any kind, including early learning, have all but vanished.*

Question: *I want to ask about the proportion of money coming to the young. I have heard statistics on television that an older person can expect five times as much help as a young child in terms of federal funding. Is that true?*

Answer: *I believe that is true. I did not mention before that the federal money which is used for the support of day care for children comes primarily from the Title XX amendments to the social security law. These amendments provide funding for a whole range of social services, of which day care for children is only one. Children's programs often find themselves in competition with other needed services, including senior citizen centers, for use of the same scarce federal dollars. In looking at the way in which public funds for human services are spent, it is important to remember that the elderly, unlike children, represent a voting constituency which is organized and active politically.*

Question: *I have been observing some day care centers in which the children remain until 6 p.m. Some of them seem to be pretty barren places, just a little beyond custodial. To me there should be a lot more stimuli. For example, one of my students is starting to build a day-care center and I offered to bring over a little television so that the children could watch* Sesame Street *at 3 or 4 o'clock in the afternoon, when they are tired. They'll learn productive language, at least, from watching* Sesame Street. *They don't do it all day but they could gain something from watching at selected times.*

Answer: *Who is going to see to it that they don't watch television all day?*

Question: *I hope the teacher will put it away, perhaps in a closet, and bring it out again at 3:30 p.m. It seems that would be fun for the children.*

Answer: *Television, properly used, can be a valuable classroom tool. Some centers do have sets and use them for this purpose.*

Question: *Well, there are a lot of people who won't allow television at all. I mean, it's a no-no. But there are some things which can be learned from the television.*

Answer: *A few centers do have television sets and, I hope, use them judiciously. However, one of the reasons why a whole philosophy has grown up against television in the classroom is the fact that often the director or supervisor can't control the teacher's use of it. We did talk about the dangers of the electronic age, but that did not include the possibility that a teacher may be tempted, on occasion, to use the classroom television to "sneak-a-peek" at his or her favorite soap opera while children are present instead of concentrating on her obligation to provide the children with learning experiences which are both appropriate and participatory rather than passive.*

Chapter 10

School Influences on the Language of Children

Bryant Fillion

Fordham University

Few predetermined events so change the lives of children as their induction into formal education. Even for those children who have spent 1 or more years in some form of day care, "starting school" in kindergarten or first grade is an important occasion in their lives, the beginning of an experience that will profoundly influence and perhaps dominate their lives for the next 10 to 20 years. Virtually every aspect of children's lives is touched by schooling, including—and perhaps most conspicuously—their language. No account of children's language development is complete without reference to the influence of schooling.

The school's influence on children and their language begins long before they actually arrive there. School-oriented families may begin preparing their children for school when the youngsters are still toddlers, and virtually all families anticipate that the start of schooling will mark a change in their routines. From age 3 or 4 onward, most children are aware of school as a topic of conversation, a subject of play, and an important part of the world to find out about. For most parents, education is a primary concern in thoughts about their children's future, although parents' attitudes toward school, and the importance they attach to it, may vary considerably. From a very early age, children's linguistic development is often assessed by parents and researchers alike in terms of its implications for the child's eventual academic success or failure. Given the importance of school to the children, their families, and society, it could hardly be otherwise.

Before early language development became the subject of serious educational concern and research, schools tended to view beginning pupils as linguistically naïve, and many still do. Overlooking the obvious accomplishments of children in learning to speak and understand the language of their communities, the children's preschool experiences with language, and their demonstrated facility as language learners, school programs and instruction often treat children as if they know nothing about language, especially written language, or how to learn it. This can lead to two problems: failure to exploit and build on children's strengths and experiences, and failure to appreciate the difficulty of school tasks for which many children are unprepared. According to Margaret Donaldson (1978), the failure of schools to bridge the gap between children's early experiences with language and educational demands for abstract thinking explains in large part "how something that begins so well can often end so badly":

> We are faced now with something of a puzzle. In the first few years at school all appears to go very well. The children seem eager, lively, happy. There is commonly an atmosphere of spontaneity in which they are encouraged to explore and discover and create. . . . However, when we consider what has happened by the time the children reach adolescence, we are forced to recognize that the promise of the early years frequently remains unfulfilled. Large numbers leave school with the bitter taste of defeat in them, not having mastered even moderately well those basic skills which society demands, much less having become people who rejoice in the exercise of creative intelligence. (pp. 13–14)

The lively spontaneity that Donaldson attributes to early education is far from universal, but it is unquestionably the case that at some point in schooling things go very badly wrong for a great many of our children.

Through instruction, the language environments they create, and evaluations of pupils' development, schools may empower or disable their students. Jim Cummins (1986) writes of "empowering minority students," arguing that many costly educational reforms have failed to improve the schooling of minorities because the reforms did not alter the debilitating effects of the children's "dominated" status in the society. Many minority children fail to achieve in school because, like society at large, the schools disable them by maintaining and confirming their inferior, subservient roles and attitudes that are inimical to learning and achievement. Cummins argues convincingly that to improve minority students' academic performance, the schools must provide the security, status, and power denied them by the rest of society, by (a) accepting and incorporating their language and culture into the school program, (b) encouraging the minority community's active participation in the school and their children's education, (c) promoting children's active use of language in learning, through a "reciprocal interaction-oriented" program, rather than the traditional "transmission-oriented" teaching, and (d) using assessment to advocate minority students' potential, rather than to legitimize their failures. According to Cummins, educational intervention will inevitably fail if it maintains the dominated position of minority children by confirming that the problems are their own, needing remediation, rather than problems in the system itself. Especially in the early grades it seems crucial that schools complement and build on children's previous experiences with language and language learning.

School Language Instruction

As the articles in this volume indicate, children arrive at school from a great many backgrounds and at very different stages of linguistic development. Their homes, communities, and day-care experiences all influence children's language learning and use, their attitudes toward and expectations of school, and, to varying degrees, the school's expectations of them. Although by the time they start school virtually all children have achieved an impressive degree of communicative competence within their linguistic communities, they differ considerably in the range of language uses that they command confidently and in their knowledge of the world, which is the concern of schooling.

In addition to linguistic and knowledge differences, there is considerable variation in the children's readiness to be taught in the ways that schools are prepared to teach. School practices such as those advocated in this book by Wells and Bissex, emphasizing the meaning-negotiation and development of insight by which children initially learn language, are still relatively rare, and traditional school practices pose serious learning problems for a great many youngsters. As Ann Haas Dyson's (1984) research suggests, children's language-learning problems in school may result as much from the type of instruction they receive as from deficiencies in their linguistic development. Dyson's studies of individual pupils demonstrate how the completion of teacher-imposed literacy tasks may involve "learning to do school" more than learning language, and may, in fact, inhibit genuine language development (Fillion & Brause, 1987).

The differences between language instruction at home and at school have been discussed by Wells, Bissex, and others in this volume. In the home, the child is customarily treated as an individual and as a member of a family, which may or may not be especially concerned with formal education. In homes and day-care institutions, "care" is the primary concern, with instruction secondary, generally informal, and often in response to the individual child's interests, activities, and developmental agenda. In school, the child is treated primarily as a learner, a passive recipient of teaching, and a member of a class of pupils constituted primarily for purposes of instruction. Whereas language and learning in the home are frequently initiated by the child and generally occur in situations that help children comprehend the meaning of what is said and done, language and learning in school are usually initiated and controlled by adults, and tend to be less related to immediate circumstances. This situation is different and imposing even if the child has had experiences in day-care classes because, at least in most schools, the task structures are so very different.

In school, instruction becomes a primary concern, and in most schools instruction is explicit, structured, and imposed, however tactfully and humanely, as a set of performance demands. The knowledge and skills to be learned are usually determined, for the teacher and the children, by a curriculum, rather than by circumstances or by the learner's interests. The more explicit and extensive the curriculum demands become, the less time and energy there is for work on child-initiated learning.

In societies such as ours, it is not surprising that schooling is becoming increasingly technologized and programmed. Through the development of instructional materials and teaching practices, education and its support industries strive to find the most efficient and effective ways to "deliver instruction" to the large numbers of children in the "system." Following the analogy of medicine, education has tried to conduct and apply instructional research so that teaching becomes more of a science than an art. Children and their language are "diagnosed," often in very technical and precise ways, so that appropriate materials, tasks, and activities may be "prescribed" as "treatments." Especially for children who have difficulty learning in school, instruction is generally viewed as a way to "remedy" their deficiencies rather than as a means of helping them build on their strengths.

One effect of making instruction more precise and technical is that teachers are encouraged to become educational technicians as well as, or instead of, facilitators of learning. Technical knowledge for teachers places primary emphasis on teaching, rather than learning: familiarity with and skill in using various machines, programs, and structured procedures for instruction and evaluation. For many teachers, especially in the elementary schools, demands for technical proficiency create frustration and stress, especially if the school's concern with procedures appears to outweigh concern for its students. As in the medical profession itself, there is controversy in education about the extent to which practitioners should rely on intuitive judgments and personal interaction with pupils, rather than on objective measurements and prescribed procedures. Within schools, "ordinary" classroom teachers may hesitate to question the expertise of certified specialists in reading or special education, especially when such experts possess demonstrable technical skills. Perhaps the most common, and understandable reaction to such expertise is to let the experts handle the problems without giving much thought to whether technical expertise is really necessary or warranted.

Another effect of increasingly technical instruction is that parents may be further excluded from the educational process. As teaching becomes more technical and specialized, parental reluctance to participate, aid, question, or intervene may also increase, in much the same way that laypeople hesitate to question the expertise of medical doctors. There is already a pronounced tendency in many communities for parents to turn their children's education over to schools, and then to stand back and go on about their adult lives. In fact, most challenges to the school's authority result from arguments about what is taught (such as sex education, or evolution) rather than from what students fail to learn. Communities may become vocal when particular schools produce standardized test results below national or local norms, but the usual reaction is to demand more expert intervention rather than, as in the case of disputed curriculum areas, to question how things are to be done.

Despite the accumulating evidence that schools have at best a marginal record of success in achieving their stated goals with the majority of students, and a record of near-failure with particular minorities, most parents are unwilling to intervene or to question the school's judgments about their children. How is a layperson to dispute expert's judgments based on sophisticated tests and diagnostic procedures that demonstrate conclusively that the problem lies with the child and not in the system itself?

Systematic, structured teaching of language, with emphasis on discrete skill instruction, is a natural response to criticism of schools in a society that places great faith in technology. If careful, systematic, step-by-step planning can conquer outer space and disease, surely such approaches can conquer ignorance and illiteracy. Direct, part-to-whole teaching is also an extension of the traditional teacher-centered, transmission-oriented classroom. However, instead of transmitting content—information about language—today's teacher is more apt to set "skill-developing tasks" intended to increase pupils' command of specific processes considered necessary for the larger acts of reading and writing. As Harvard linguist Courtney Cazden observed in 1977:

> Responding to real or imagined community pressures, able and conscientious teachers all over the country are providing abundant practice in discrete basic skills; while classrooms where children are integrating those skills in the service of exciting speaking, listening, reading, and writing activities are becoming rare exceptions. (p. 41)

Despite the logic, attractiveness, and increasing use of such approaches, however, they are not universally accepted or endorsed, either by teachers or researchers. Whereas much classroom research correlating teaching practices to students' test performance tends to support systematic, direct instruction, especially with lower SES students, researchers in children's language development generally favor more "natural," student-centered, progressive methods, especially in early reading and writing. As Fillion and Brause (1987) observe: "This disparity among pedagogical prescriptions resulting from different kinds of research is one of the most interesting problems in language education today."

The underlying question is whether longstanding, conventional patterns of schooling should be accepted as given and probably unchangeable, or whether alternative patterns that exploit children's preschool experiences and learning should be attempted. At issue is whether instruction should be a more precisely and efficiently programmed version of present practices, or more like the interactional, responsive practices in homes that successfully prepare children for literacy and schooling. The question is more complex than it may appear, because the criteria for assessing home practices and their outcomes include the children's successful learning in the very school conditions that are being challenged.

To what extent should "the ability to learn well from conventional teaching" be a criterion of successful development? Is the possible inappropriateness of such learning for language development a ground for dismissing it as an objective? The dilemma is similar to those posed by Donaldson (1978) and, in this volume, by Hedley. Donaldson argues that "disembedded," abstract thinking is difficult and perhaps unnatural for many adults and children, and accounts in large part for school failures; "when we set such store by disembedded modes of thought we make the pursuit of education in our society a difficult enterprise for the human mind—one which many minds refuse at an early age" (p. 81). Nevertheless, she argues, such thinking is a prerequisite for mastery of any formal system of knowledge, thus a highly valued and necessary skill, and a legitimate objective of schooling: "The better you are at tackling problems without having to be sustained by human sense, the more likely you are to succeed in our educational system, the more you will be approved of and loaded with prizes" (pp. 77–78). Similarly, Hedley argues that early childhood workers' legitimate rejection of traditional language teaching methods as inappropriate for young children does not justify their rejection of written language and literacy in preschool programs. Among the benefits of children's early introduction to written language is that they will perform better when they are finally subjected to the traditional methods.

Given that language development seems to occur naturally, at least for young children, in any environment that provides models of language behavior and opportunities for children to use language, is instruction really necessary? Bereiter and Scardamalia (1982) address this issue in discussing the role of instruction in writing pedagogy:

> Since we are dealing with a developmental process [i.e., writing] . . . the question naturally arises why it should be necessary to intervene instructionally at all. If proper conditions for developmental experience were provided, wouldn't things take care of themselves? . . .
>
> Let us agree that in a society where a high premium was placed on written composition skills, and where everyone was expected to display competence in them, natural learning would probably take care of the problems [in composing skill] we have been wrestling with. . . . *But if such situations could be created freely, there would be no writing problem, at least not as we know it. It is precisely because conditions for learning to write are generally so unfavorable that natural development stands in need of considerable assistance.*
>
> . . . the level of mastery that the social environment supports is quite a bit short of what the culture actually seems to need. That is, development does go on in comprehension, analytical, and compositional skills, but in the end most citizens don't reach anything like the level that a liberal democratic philosophy deems desirable. (emphasis added)

Given the difficulty Bereiter and Scardamalia suggest of altering environments, immediate improvements in language education will probably depend largely on improving instruction. Nevertheless, as all studies of language development confirm, the environment plays a crucial role.

Schools as Language Environments

Schools influence children's language, not only through the nature and content of instruction, but also through the linguistic environments they create. Schools, like homes and day-care agencies, provide children with examples of language use from which to learn, and, even more explicitly than most homes, they control the children's own uses of language by determining what linguistic behaviors will be encouraged, demanded, ignored, or discouraged. Since schools provide a larger and more varied language community than most children have experienced in their preschool years, they presumably present expanded opportunities for language observation, use, and learning. As Halliday (1973) and others have complained, however, the range of language uses modeled and encouraged by schools is generally far more restricted than what children have experienced at home, and there is an overwhelming emphasis on reading, often to the virtual exclusion of speech and writing.

Strangely enough, one glaring example of schools' restrictions on children's language is in its use for learning. Both in and out of school, learning often involves and occurs through language and provides powerful motivation for continued linguistic development. Children discussing their toys or problems with friends and secondary students exploring concepts in essays for their teachers are all involved both in shaping their understanding and in extending their language resources to accomplish personally significant ends. As Britton (1970), Barnes (1976), and other language theorists have noted, language is a primary means by which people construct their mental representations of reality, and they do so through talk and writing as much as by listening and reading (Fillion, 1985). Given the importance of active language uses in learning, it is surprising that such uses are typically more limited in schools, where learning is a primary concern, than they are in the home. As numerous studies indicate, the most active language user in most classrooms is the teacher rather than the learner. In most classrooms, if children are to reformulate the information presented to them into knowledge, they must do so silently, in their heads. The silent learning environment in most schools stands in sharp contrast to the lively child–adult interactions cited in Wells's studies of homes.

Some of the most important differences between homes and schools as language environments are summarized in the chart below. Characteristics listed in the *Schools* column refer primarily to classroom instruction time. During recess, on the playground, in the lunch room, and in other noninstructional situations, schools are often linguistically similar to home environments, with the notable exception that there are more children present and adults often function as supervisors rather than as participants.

Differences in Home and School Language Environments

Homes	*Schools*
Adults are known personally by the children	Adults are known in their professional roles
Children usually from similar backgrounds and circumstances	Children from a wide range of backgrounds and circumstances
Frequent opportunity for child–adult interaction, one-to-one	Limited opportunity for child–adult interaction
Children observe adults using language purposefully for a wide range of reasons	Much adult language use directed to or intended for children for instructional purposes (Most adult to adult language in schools is conducted in private.)
Varying opportunity for privacy	Limited opportunity for privacy
Emphasis on oral language, for an extensive and increasing range of purposes	Emphasis on written language, primarily reading, mainly for academic purposes

Homes	*Schools*
Children ask questions and express opinions	Children answer teachers' questions and keep opinions to themselves
Children's reading and writing activities perhaps encouraged but generally voluntary	Reading and writing activities required, scheduled, and usually structured by adults
Adults collaborate with, encourage, and generally appreciate children's uses of language, including self-expression	Adults require, give instructions about, and evaluate children's language uses, often discouraging self-expression
Most language situationally relevant; elements of the non-language context help children to make sense of the language	Most language, at least in lessons, unrelated to the immediate situational context
Children initiate much language interaction with adults, often determining the content	Adults initiate most interactions and control the content, especially in lessons
Language content determined by circumstances or concerns of individuals involved	Language content determined by the curriculum or instructional concerns of teachers
Personal, private, and social concerns discussed with adults as well as other children	Personal, private, social concerns increasingly limited to out-of-classroom occasions, with adults absent
Children's language ability observed and assessed informally, unobtrusively, and usually unthreateningly	Language abilities explicitly and formally evaluated, often producing anxiety

Even though specific differences among individual homes and schools may be less pronounced than these general ones, homes and schools are distinctly different environments. They provide children with very different examples of, demands for, and opportunities to use language, and they usually require very different ways of learning. Obviously, not all homes are productive language-learning environments, and all schools are not inhibiting environments. For language educators, the criterion to be used in assessing any environment is whether or not it promotes children's linguistic development in desirable ways.

Educational judgments about language environments and language instruction depend heavily on our theories about how language develops and is influenced. At least since the mid-1960s, a mainstream theoretical stance has dominated the professional literature on English education. Fillion and Brause (1987) delineate that stance as follows:

> It contains several related beliefs, the most basic of which is that virtually all children have a natural facility with language learning that we have failed to recognize or exploit in our schools and classrooms. In a culture where written language is prominent and readily available, basic literacy is a natural extension of an individual's linguistic development, given adequate environmental conditions. Language facility, written as well as oral, develops primarily through personally meaningful, active uses of

> language in service of genuine human intentions, including the intention to learn: to build an adequate cognitive representation of the world. Teachers and schools can best influence students' language development by facilitating their intentional use of language, oral and written, for a wide range of personal, social, and academic purposes, rather than by drilling students in predetermined sequences of discrete skills apart from their significant use, or by teaching information about language. Students' language—vocalized, written, or as inner speech—plays, or should play a significant part in virtually all mental activity and school learning, and these language uses not only promote better learning but linguistic and cognitive development as well. Following from these beliefs is the contention that the language environment in many existing classrooms is "unnatural," and detrimentally so, in that students are diverted from participation in meaningful language acts and events in which they would otherwise normally engage and are made to participate instead in a narrow range of structured activities and situations distinct from purposeful, significant language uses and learning.

As the articles in the present volume indicate, research in language development, including the studies of Gordon Wells, Denny Taylor, and Glenda Bissex, have tended to support and elaborate this mainstream theory. Janet Emig (1983) summarizes the research on writing development and draws the following educational implications from it, noting that none of the implied conditions is met in current school programs:

1. Although writing is natural, it is activated by enabling environments.
2. These environments have the following characteristics: They are safe, structured, private, unobtrusive, and literate.
3. Adults in these environments have two special roles: They are fellow practitioners, and they are providers of possible content, experiences, and feedback.
4. Children need frequent opportunities to practice writing, many of these playful. (p. 139)

Frank Smith (1983) would support Emig's list but add emphasis to her third point, stressing the importance of "demonstrations" that permit children to observe language in action for significant purposes. He questions the extent to which children in school ever see adults using language and thinking in personally meaningful ways. Despite such widespread support by language theorists and researchers, however, there is little instructional research to demonstrate that such guidelines can be translated into general practice on a large scale within present patterns of schooling, or that such practice would in fact produce the linguistic and cognitive results claimed for it (Fillion & Brause, 1987).

Although theorists and researchers differ considerably about how instruction and school environments should be changed, there are few defenders of the status quo. Present school environments are widely criticized for: (a) preventing children from using what they already know about language and language learning, (b) encouraging student passivity rather than active involvement and learning, (c) failing to provide tasks and activities that lead to significant development, and (d) creating misconceptions about language and what it means to "know" language. Perhaps the most serious of these misconceptions is that facility with language is the same as facility in doing the school tasks intended to develop language, a misconception shared by many programs and teachers as well as their students. Unfortunately, this misconception is also supported by many of the school's evaluation procedures.

Schools' Evaluations of Language Development

In addition to the schools' instructional and environmental influences on children's language, they also exert an influence through evaluations. Academic performance is an important yardstick by which children and their language are measured, and in a very practical sense whatever the schools emphasize and evaluate becomes important to the children, their parents, and their teachers. Through formal evaluations such as minimal competency tests for school promotion and graduation, and SATs for college entrance, all of which emphasize language, the society makes explicit the range, nature, and standards of linguistic and cognitive behavior it expects and values. Similarly, within schools the tests, tasks, assignments, and activities used to evaluate and "grade" children constitute the school's operational definition of language development. One of the earliest lessons children learn about schools, to the dismay of many teachers, is that what really matters is what is on the test.

Especially in elementary schools, teachers' holistic, impressionistic assessments of children's language development are usually based on a wide range of experiences with the children, including but not limited to observations of their performance on various instructional tasks. Nevertheless, teachers are sometimes reluctant to allow their subjective observational judgments to influence their formal grading of students, preferring to emphasize more impersonal and objective measures, such as scores on tests and tasks. Similarly, in making "official" judgments about students' achievement and development, schools and state education agencies differ widely in the relative weight they assign to formal, "objective" measures and to teachers' assessments. The great increase in state-mandated testing during the 1970s has suggested a clear preference for the former and distrust of the latter. Perhaps this is another indication of our faith in technology, that we tend to rely more on numbers produced by scientifically constructed tests than on judgments rendered by "ordinary" humans with access to a great deal more data.

The process and focus of evaluation do not just objectify the values underlying the curriculum; they exercise considerable control over teaching, what is taught, and judgments about students, including students' attitudes toward their own competence. At least from the time they enter school, children believe they are "good" at using language only when the school says they are good at it, quite apart from evidence of proficiency in their out-of-school lives. Even adults who demonstrate outstanding linguistic proficiency in their personal and professional lives often denigrate their own abilities because of remembered failures in school language tasks or on important tests.

The power of schools to render public judgment on pupils' language and learning, based largely on academic criteria, has important social as well as psychological implications. For example, Cummins (1986) stresses the role of educational assessment in legitimizing the continued disabling of many minority children:

> In some cases assessment itself may play the primary role, but more often it has been used to locate the "problem" within the minority student, thereby screening from critical scrutiny the subtractive nature of the school program, the exclusionary orientation of teachers toward minority communities, and transmission models of teaching that inhibit students from active participation in learning. (p. 29)

The underlying issue, discussed earlier in this chapter, is whether "the ability to learn well from conventional teaching" is itself a justifiable criterion of development.

In early childhood and nonacademic situations, the successful use of linguistic forms and skills for an increasing range of personal and social purposes is the usual measure of language development and proficiency. In daily living, judgments of an individual's intellectual and linguistic competence are generally based on the individual's awareness and command of world knowledge, reasonable behavior, and use of language to accomplish his or her intentions in a variety of situations. A person's ability to say what one may tacitly know about language (such as grammatical rules) is seldom observed, and the conventional "correctness" of one's language varies in importance with the situation. (Many very successful adults, including academics, speak heavily accented or nonstandard English that is considered a linguistic weakness in schoolchildren.) Using the criteria of language use and command of linguistic resources, researchers in preschool language development are consistently impressed by the amount and nature of virtually all children's language learning.

Using the school's criteria, researchers tend to express dismay at the increasing disparity in children's development, especially among those from differing ethnic and socioeconomic backgrounds. At this point, it is not clear whether such disparity is due more to actual linguistic differences in the children and their backgrounds, to the inherent difficulty of academic demands, to the inadequacy of instruction, or to limitations in schools' evaluation procedures and criteria. In school evaluations, there is a distinct emphasis on literacy to the exclusion of oral language, on abstract thought rather than everyday, practical thinking, and on academic uses of language to acquire and demonstrate skills, understandings, and knowledge defined by the school's agenda. Such linguistic proficiency, and the mental processes it implies, have unquestionable practical use and value in the society, but it is nonetheless restrictive. A great many socially valued language uses, such as for selling, managing, comforting, healing, and entertaining, are virtually ignored in most school assessments, thereby limiting the range of situations in which children can demonstrate their competence. Similarly, the schools' heavy reliance on paper-and-pencil testing, even when it is justifiable in terms of efficiency, restricts students' use or demonstration of their oral proficiency in evaluations.

To some extent, the distinctive nature of language evaluation in schools is justified by the nature and purpose of education. It is quite legitimate, for instance, for schools to assess students' mastery of particular skills and processes which may only have value as steps in learning more complex behaviors. Difficulties arise when such formative evaluations assume the importance of ends in themselves, giving children and some teachers the impression that discrete skills are the goal, rather than a means to the end of more proficient language use. The problem is illustrated in writing programs that devote so much attention to spelling, grammar, usage, and punctuation that there is virtually no opportunity for children to write. Following the logic that what is tested is important, students in such programs may understandably conclude that transcription, rather than composition, is what really matters. Unfortunately, as writing research indicates, transcription skills are seldom mastered when divorced from their significant use in the service of composing (Smith, 1982).

Fortunately for children, their parents, and society, children are extraordinarily flexible and adaptable and are often able to pursue their learning and developmental agendas even in the most unfavorable circumstances. This does not relieve parents and teachers from the responsibility of seeking to improve the instruction, environmental conditions, and evaluation procedures that influence children's language and learning. But we must not, in the process, fail to appreciate the resources and resiliency of the children themselves. We sometimes need reminding, as Denny Taylor reminds us in this book, that childhood is a unique time of life, a time to celebrate the irrational freakiness of ordinary things, and not merely a stage to be developed out of by schooling. And it is well to remember, as perfection continues to elude us, that children themselves are often the best sources of information about how to teach them.

References

Barnes, D. (1976). *From communication to curriculum*. Harmondsworth, England: Penguin.

Bereiter, C., & Scardamalia, M. (1982). From conversation to composition: The role of instruction in a developmental process. In R. Glaser (Ed.), *Advances in instructional psychology* (Vol. 2). Hillsdale, NJ: Erlbaum.

Britton, J. (1970). *Language and learning*. Harmondsworth, England: Penguin.

Cazden, C. B. (1977, October). Language, literacy, and literature: Putting it all together. *National Elementary Principal*, pp. 40–42.

Cummins, J. (1986). Empowering minority students: A framework for intervention. *Harvard Educational Review, 56*, 18–36.

Donaldson, M. (1978). *Children's minds*. London: Fontana/Croom Helm.

Dyson, A. H. (1984). Learning to write/learning to do school: Emergent writers' interpretations of school literacy tasks. *Research in the Teaching of English, 18*, 233–264.

Emig, J. (1983). *The web of meaning: Essays on writing, teaching, learning, and thinking*. Upper Montclair, NJ: Boynton/Cook.

Fillion, B. (1985). Language across the curriculum. In T. Husen & T. N. Postlethwaite (Eds.), *International Encyclopedia of Education*. Oxford: Pergamon Press.

Fillion, B., & Brause, R. S. (1987). Research into classroom practices: What have we learned and where are we going? In J. R. Squire (Ed.), *The dynamics of language learning: Research in Reading and English*. Urbana, IL: National Conference on Research in English and ERIC RCS Center.

Halliday, M. A. K. (1973). *Explorations in the functions of language*. London: Arnold.

Smith, F. (1982). *Writing and the writer*. New York: Holt, Rinehart, & Winston.

Smith, F. (1983). *Essays into literacy*. Exeter, NH: Heinemann.

Author Index

Subject Index